Look Around Lancashire

A Guide to Tourist Attractions
in Lancashire
suitable for Group and Individual Visits

Lancashire
County
Council

Look Around Lancashire

Preface

I am delighted to commend this enlarged and thoroughly revised edition of "Look Around Lancashire".

The three earlier editions have all proved to be best - sellers and have introduced the wealth of attractions which the County has to offer to residents and visitors alike. All will be surprised at the choice available.

You will be well rewarded as you "Look Around Lancashire".

David Tattersall

County Planning Officer
Lancashire County Planning Department
East Cliff County Offices
Preston PR1 3EX.

How to use "Look Around Lancashire"

"Look Around Lancashire" has the attractions grouped together in Sections and are listed in the Contents on page (iii). Each Section has its own title page, on the reverse of which is a map showing the reference number of each venue at its approximate location. The reference number is also given in the "How to get there" sub heading of each venue's description. In addition, each description also has a map showing the location in greater detail, and these should be used in conjunction with Ordnance Survey and motorists' maps and street plans.

Practical details of each facility are given including telephone numbers with the national STD code; local codes should be obtained from a Telephone Dialling Code Book or Directory Enquiries. Cellnet telephone numbers have been introduced for the first time in this edition. The numbers are obtained by dialling the codes on any telephone. Details about access to the venues by the disabled are included.

When the Schools Edition was published in 1982 all the known Town and Country Trails within the County were included but now, six years later, a greatly extended Town and Country Trails Section can only be a representative selection. The County Council and District Councils publish many leaflets on Trails and other attractions and these are available from Information Centres.

Look Around Lancashire:

Schools Edition	March 1982.
First Edition	June 1983
Second Edition	June 1984
Third Edition	July 1988

Design and artwork by County Planning Department.
Printed by Leyland Printing Company, Leyland, Lancashire.
© Lancashire County Planning Department 1988

The maps used in this book which are based upon the Ordnance Survey map are reproduced with the permission of the Controller of Her Majesty's Stationery Office. Crown copyright reserved.

ISBN 0 902228 722

Contents

continued......

Leisure Parks

Picnic Sites

Historic Houses and Castles

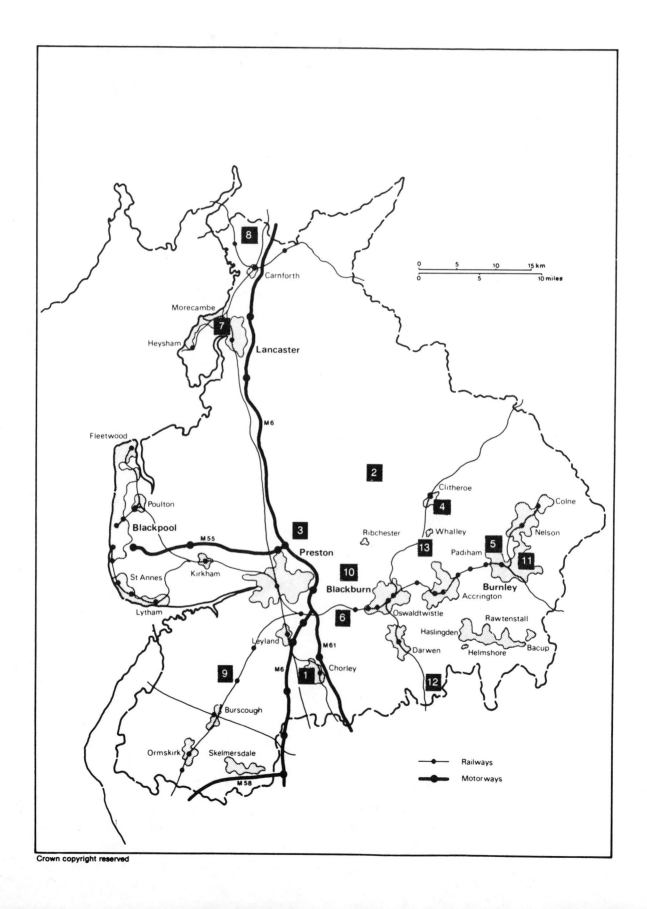

Astley Hall

THE CROMWELL BED

Elizabethan Hall, dating originally from about 1580, built around a central courtyard and an example of English Renaissance work, rebuilt in Jacobean manner in 1666. The Hall is furnished largely in the manner of Late Tudor and Early Stuart England (1580-1656) and includes two unique items worthy of special mention - an Elizabethan bed known locally as the Cromwell Bed; and a famous shovel-board table in the Long Gallery. Museum exhibits with collections of pottery (extensive collection of Leeds Pottery), paintings, horse brasses and lead soldiers. There is also an Art Gallery where regular and varied exhibitions are held. The Drawing Room has been refurnished as a period room displaying early 18th century English walnut furniture. Guided tours, lectures, etc., can be arranged free of charge. Astley Park, in which the Hall is located, extends to 105 acres and contains well-wooded walks with footbridge across the River Chor. There is a wide range of outdoor attractions - children's playground, paddling pool, pets corner, tennis courts, bowling greens, putting green, woodland walk and nature trail.

Open: April-September: Daily 12 noon to 6pm October-March: Monday-Friday 12 noon-4pm Saturday 10am-4pm Sunday 11am-4pm

Booking Requirements: Advance booking required for parties. Tours and lectures need prior arrangement.

Admission Charges: A charge is made for admission.

How to get there 1

Address: Astley Hall Museum and Art Gallery, Astley Park, Chorley.

Contact: The Amenities Officer, Amenities Department, Public Baths, Union Street, Chorley PR7 1AB. Tel:Chorley (02572) 65611 or 62166 (Astley Hall).

Location: Main entrance in Park Road, (A6), Chorley. Signposted from all main roads in Chorley. Free leaflet detailing how to get there available on request.

Ordnance Survey Grid Reference: SD 574 183.

Parking: Large free car park at the rear of the Hall.

Public Transport: Main entrance situated within 1/2 mile of Chorley bus and railway stations. For details enquire: Buses - Chorley 62247 (Travel Sales Offices, New Market Street); Trains - Chorley station - Chorley 62616.

Facilities

Catering and Picnicking: Light refreshments available at the cafe, a converted coach-house, next to the Hall. The Hall is situated in a large park with extensive grass areas for picnicking purposes and picnic tables have been provided.

Toilets: Toilet facilities are available in the coach-house adjacent to the Hall.

Shelter: There are no additional indoor facilities for wet weather.

Disabled: There are no lifts to the upper floors. There is a toilet for disabled persons and a garden for the blind is sited near the entrance to the Park.

Average Length of Time Taken: Half day trip around Museum and Art Gallery combined with picnic lunch and outdoor activities.

Miscellaneous Information: It is possible to arrange a period costume display by members of the Astley Hall Society. The Society makes a small charge for this service which includes entrance to the Hall, the balance plus any donation is used for the direct benefit of Astley Hall.

Leaflets/Books/Guides Available: Yes.

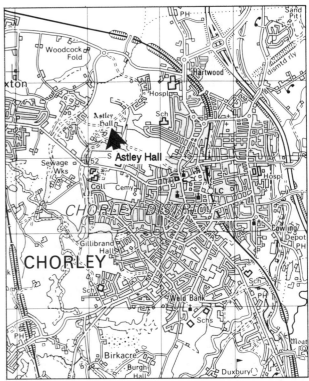

Crown copyright reserved

3

Browsholme Hall

Set amongst some of the finest countryside in the north west is this beautiful example of an unspoilt Tudor Country House, one of the most historic mansions in the Ribble Valley. This has been the family seat of the Parkers, Bowbearers of the Forest of Bowland, since 1507 and the family still live here and show visitors around. The Hall is surrounded by trees and extensive gardens and is famous for its fine oak panelling, pictures, armour, family treasures and much of the original furniture. There is a remarkable series of family portraits including works by Devis, Romney, Northcote and Batoni.

Admission Charges: A charge is made for admission. Reductions for organised parties.

Open: 2pm to 5pm on Easter Saturday and the week end following; every Saturday in June, July, August; late Spring Bank Holiday weekend; Summer Bank Holiday and the preceding week; organised parties at other times by arrangement.

How to get there 2

Address: Browsholme Hall, Clitheroe, Lancashire BB7 3DE.

Contact: Mrs.Parker. Tel:Stonyhurst (025 486) 330.

Location: Five miles north-west of Clitheroe and two miles north of Bashall Eaves, close to the Trough of Bowland. Leave Clitheroe by the Edisford Bridge road (do not go through Waddington). From Whalley follow the Mitton/Whitewell road. From Preston follow the B6243 to Longridge, Hurst Green and Angerham then take the road to Bashall Eaves and Whitewell.

Ordnance Survey Grid Reference: SD 684 452.

Parking: Free parking at owner's risk. Entrance for cars and coaches by Lower Lodge.

Public Transport: There is an infrequent service between Clitheroe and Slaidburn, which passes the entrance to Browsholme Hall. For further details phone Ribble Travel Offices, Clitheroe (0200) 23028.

Facilities

Catering: Tea or coffee can be provided for parties if booked in advance. Picnic area. Home-made after-noon teas at Bashall Eaves Post Office (1 mile). Several local public houses serving bar lunches. Bookings for parties essential.

Toilets: Yes, within the House.

Shelter: Within the House.

Disabled: It is possible for wheelchairs to be accommodated within the building, and toilet facilities are available in the private areas of the Hall, on request.

Average Length of Stay: The guided tour of the Hall takes 45 minutes.

Group Size: Up to 55 persons.

Miscellaneous: Lake trout fishing. Day tickets available from the Water Bailiff. Tel:Stonyhurst (025 486) 605.

Leaflets/Books/Guides Available: An illustrated Guide on Browsholme Hall.

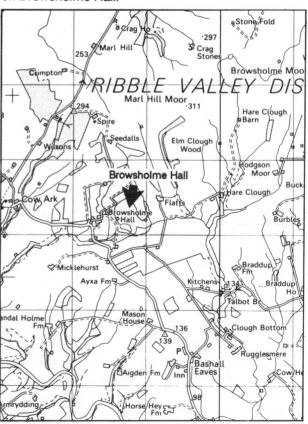

Chingle Hall

Built by Adam de Singleton in 1260, adjacent to the Viking village of Goosnargh. The Hall is a small moated Manor House with a Chapel and three Priest Hides. The Battle of Preston raged around the Hall and Oliver Cromwell reputedly climbed the chimney to espy the disposition of Royalist forces. During the Reformation it became a secret Mass Centre. It was the birthplace of Saint John Wall in 1620 who was hanged, drawn and quartered in 1679 at Worcester. He was one of the last priests to be executed for his faith, and his head is believed to be concealed in Chingle Hall. Cardinal Heenan and the Bishop of Lancaster held their historic Ecumenical meeting at Chingle Hall in 1962. An archaelogical excavation is in progress with the long term intention of uncovering the secrets of the site and its earlier dwellings. The moat when excavated will be restored to its former glory. Chingle Hall also has the reputation of being one of the most haunted houses in Britain.

Open: Daily 10am - 6pm, except Christmas and New Year's Day. Evening tours by prior arrangement only.

Booking Requirements: Coach parties to book in advance.

Admission Charge: A charge is made.

How to get there 3

Location: North east of Preston. North of the M6/M55 interchange (Junction 32 and 1), follow A6 to Broughton crossroads. Turn right (east) onto B5269 for Whittingham/Goosnargh/Longridge and after 2 miles turn right off B5269 for the Hall.

Ordnance Survey Grid Reference: SD 557 358.

Parking: Yes.

Public Transport: Ribble bus services from Preston bus station.

Facilities

Catering: Refreshments available. Picnic area.

Toilets: None

Shelter: Indoors

Disabled: Ground floor easily accessed but no special facilities within the Hall.

Amount of Time Taken: Guided tour approximately 1 hour

Group Size: Approximately 20 at a time. Additional permanent facilities are being developed which will increase the scope for group visits.

Leaflets/Books/Guides Available: Yes.

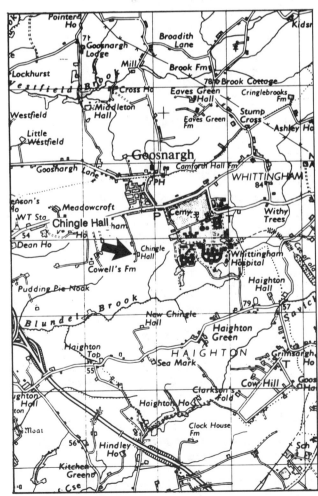

Clitheroe Castle Museum

Remains of a 12th century stronghold on a lofty mound providing wide views of the surrounding area. There are Civil War associations. The Castle is set in extensive grounds containing children's playground, bowls, tennis and refreshments. Reputed to be one of the oldest stone structures in Lancashire and has one of the smallest Norman Keeps in England. Magnificent views over the Ribble Valley bounded on the west and south by the hills of Bowland and the east by Pendle Hill. The Museum is located in Castle House, adjacent to the Castle. Exhibits in the Museum are of immense local interest - local archaeology with finds from the Ribble Valley; varied collection of carboniferous limestone fossils; aspects of the history of the ancient Borough of Clitheroe illustrated through objects, photographs, plans and documents; trades and crafts of the area with a variety of tools and equipment and reconstructed cloggers' and printers' workshops; domestic life with a wide range of household objects. Listen to the printer and clogger talking about their crafts and hear what housework was like in an Edwardian kitchen.

Opening Times: April, May and October 1.30-5pm. June to September and Bank Holiday weekends 11am-5pm.

Booking Requirements: Plenty of warning required for large parties.

Admission Charges: A charge is made for admission.

How to get there ▪4▪

Address: Clitheroe Castle Museum, Castle House, Clitheroe BB7 1BA.

Contact: Custodian, Tel:Clitheroe (0200) 24635.

Location: The Museum is prominently situated on Castle Hill in the centre of Clitheroe at the junction of Castle Street, Moor Lane and Parson Lane.

Ordnance Survey Grid Reference: SD 741 417.

Parking: Car parking is available within easy walking distance in Station Road, Railway View and Lowergate.

Public Transport: Buses stop in the town centre with services to Accrington, Blackburn and Burnley.

Facilities

Catering: Bowling green cafe open afternoons. Castle grounds suitable for picnics.

Toilets: Available in the Castle grounds.

Disabled: Access limited.

Amount of Time Taken: Approximately 1 hour, plus Castle grounds.

Group Size: Schools and parties contact the Custodian.

Leaflets/Books/Guides Available: A Guide to Clitheroe Castle.

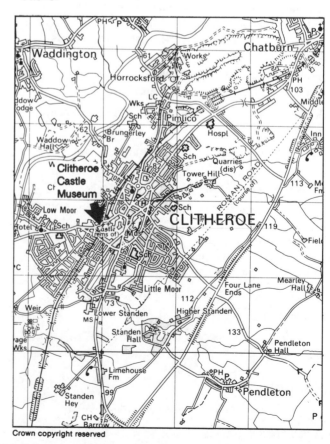

Crown copyright reserved

Gawthorpe Hall

Built between 1600 and 1605, it was designed by one of the most celebrated architects of the day. Robert Smythson, and is one of the finest Jacobean houses in the north west. The Great Hall, Drawing Room and Long Gallery are especially noteworthy. The house was given to the National Trust by the Shuttleworth family (whose home it had been for over 400 years) in 1970 and is leased to Lancashire County Council. Refurbished 1986 in the style designed for it by Sir Charles Barrie in the 1850s. Houses the famous Rachel Kay-Shuttleworth Collections of Embroidery, Lace and Costume, the largest of their kind outside London. The nationally renowned displays are supported by a comprehensive library. Outstation of the National Portrait Gallery and contains important collection of 17th century portraits. Exhibitions by professional artists and craftsmen are held in the Hall and in the Coach House Gallery. The Gallery also offers regularly changing shows of craft work for sale as well as housing a National Trust Shop. Restoration of the Great Barn (built at the same time as the Hall) and of the Loft Gallery (which forms part of the imposing Estate Block) have provided a performance area, a new setting for exhibitions and workshops and a team room.

Opening Times: April to 30 October on Tuesday, Wednesday, Thursday, Saturday and Sunday from 2pm-6pm (including Bank Holiday Mondays). The Craft Gallery and National Trust Shop open mid February to Christmas, Tuesday to Friday and Bank Holiday Mondays 10.30am-12.30pm, 2pm-5pm; Saturday and Sunday 2-5pm.

Admission Charges: A charge is made for admission. Party visits which include a guided tour must be booked in advance. Admission to the Coach House Craft Gallery and gardens is free.

How to get there 5

Address: Gawthorpe Hall, Padiham, Near Burnley BB12 8UA.

Contact: Publicity Officer, Gawthorpe Hall. Tel:Padiham (0282) 78511.

Location: Gawthorpe lies on the north side of the A671 Burnley Road, just outside Padiham centre.

Ordnance Survey Grid Reference: SD 807 342.

Parking: Yes.

Public Transport: Buses from Burnley, Colne, Nelson and Preston pass the end of the drive.

Facilities

Catering: Tea room.

Toilets: Yes.

Disabled: May be set down at the front door and can see Entrance Hall and two principal rooms without having to climb stairs. Toilet facilities.

Length of Time Taken: General trip 1 1/2 hours - longer for more specialised study.

Group Size: Party bookings for up to 45, to take place between 11am-2pm.

Miscellaneous Information: Facilities are available for individual private study or research on items in the Rachel Kay-Shuttleworth Collections. These are available at a charge of £5 per day for adults and £2 per day for bonafide full-time students. Students under 18 can use these facilities free of charge. For full details contact the curator.

Leaflets/books/Guides Available: Yes.

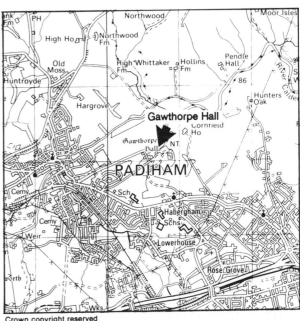

Crown copyright reserved

Hoghton Tower

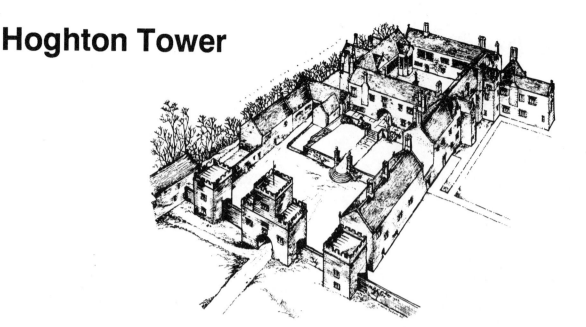

Fortified 16th century hill top mansion 700 feet above sea level. Ancestral home of the 'de Hoghton' family since William the Conqueror. Banqueting Hall where the "Loin of Beef" was knighted by King James I in 1617. The King's Bedchamber, Audience Chamber, Ballroom and other state rooms used by the King, the Duke of Buckingham and other nobles in his suite, still perfectly preserved. Tudor Well House with its horse-drawn pump and oaken windlass and the Stone Cells which housed malefactors and cattle thieves. Walled gardens, lawns and Old English Rose Garden. Walks and grounds with views of the neighbouring moors, hills of the Lake District and Welsh mountains. Permanent exhibition of historic Hoghton documents. Dolls Houses; Tea Room, Souvenir and Gift Shop. Guided tours possible.

Opening Times: Easter Saturday, Sunday and Monday; every Sunday until end of October; Saturday and Sunday during July and August; all Bank Holidays 2pm to 5pm. Guided tours for parties of 20 and more during the day or any evening of the week by prior arrangement.

Booking Requirements: It is advisable to book all group visits well in advance.

Admission Charges: A charge is made for admission.

How to get there 6

Address: Hoghton Tower, Hoghton, Preston PR5 0SH.

Contact: The Administrator. Tel.Hoghton (025485) 2986 during the day.

Location: Situated off the A675 Blackburn Old Road, half-way between Preston and Blackburn, 5 miles from both.

Ordnance Survey Grid Reference: SD 622 264.

Parking: Ample coach and car parking.

Public Transport: Half-hourly bus service from Preston and Blackburn to entrance gates.

Facilities

Catering: Self-service Tea Rooms (afternoon teas, snacks, light refreshments, ices, soft drinks, sweets).

Special catering by arrangement. The Tilting Green is excellent for picnics.

Toilets: Yes.

Shelter: On school visits picnics may be brought into the tea room if the weather is wet.

Disabled: There are too many stairs for wheelchairs to be accommodated but handicapped and blind persons are helped. Access to ground floor, but need to be notified in advance.

Average Length of Time Taken: 1 1/2 to 2hours.

Group Size: 20 minimum.

Leaflets/Books/Guides: Yes.

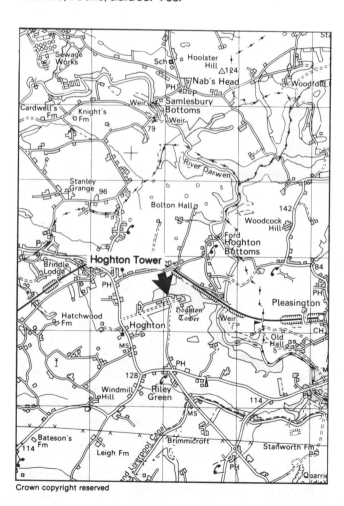

Lancaster Castle

Originally a Norman Fortress built in the 11th century on the site of a Roman Military Fort. The Keep still dates from this time and the upper parts and the Beacon Turret were restored in 1585. The Castle was twice strengthened before this and all the building can still be seen. The Castle has been used as a prison and law-court since 1196. Visitors can see the beautiful Shire Hall with large pointed windows and elaborate interior decoration. The Crown Court and Grand Jury room are included in the tour. The Drop Room is interesting, being the room where prisoners were pinioned before being led out to Hanging Corner, and a tour of the dungeons is included. Many Lancashire Witches were tried and hanged in the Castle. *Due to extensive repairs being undertaken the Grand Jury Room and Drop Room are not available in 1988. Crown Court sittings during 1988 will restrict the tour to the Shire Hall, Hadrian's Tower and Dungeons with the Crown Court/Barristers' libraries when not in use.*

Opening Times: Open to the public for guided tours only, from Good Friday to 30 September from 10.30am until 4pm although times of the last tour will vary according to the season. Closed Mondays in 1988 except Bank Holidays.

Booking Requirements: It is necessary for large parties to book in advance. Guided tours only are available, no lectures are given but further information about the Castle can be obtained prior to the visit by contacting the Castle Keeper.

Admission Charges: Two different tours are available depending on whether Courts are in session, at which times the Crown Court is omitted from the tour. A charge is made for either a full or part tour.

How to get there   7

Address: Shire Hall, Castle Parade, Lancaster LA1 1YJ.

Contact: The Castle Keeper. Tel:Lancaster (0524) 64998.

Location: to the north west of Lancaster City centre south of the River Lune. From the A6 - the main road running through Lancaster (one way system) - turn left at the junction with Meeting House Lane and first right opposite the GPO. This road leads to the Castle gates. Lancaster is approached from the north and south on the A6 or M6 and Lancaster railway station is located on the main north-south line.

Ordnance Survey Grid Reference: SD 473 619.

Parking: Is available outside the Castle and Priory Walls but the time is limited. A multi-storey car park is located 200 yards away to the north, opposite which is a coach park for longer stays.

Public Transport: Regular trains to the north and south on the main line through Lancaster. Connections at Preston for all other areas. Hourly bus service from Preston and Kendal to Lancaster bus station (5 minutes walk to Castle). Good local bus services within Lancaster and outlying districts to the City centre.

Facilities

Catering: None, but there are catering facilities in the adjacent Priory and picnicking is possible in its grounds.

Toilets: These are limited and with no disabled facilities.

Shelter: The tour is indoors.

Disabled: No special facilities but help is given to enable disabled people to enjoy a visit.

Length of Visit: Tours lasting approximately 1 hour. Visits can also be made to the adjacent Priory Church and grounds.

Group Size: Minimum 10 - 50 maximum.

Leaflets/Books/Guides: Yes.

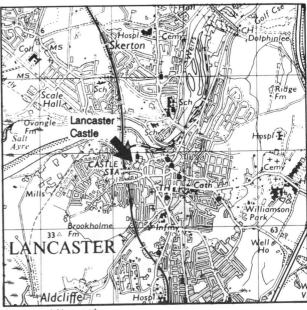

Crown copyright reserved

9

Leighton Hall

A beautifully situated country house, first built in 1246 and destroyed by government troops in 1715. Rebuilt in 1760 with a neo-gothic facade added in 1825. On display are fine examples of early Gillow furniture, paintings by Seago, Morland and others; silver and objets d'art and a collection of early French and English clocks. The grounds are open to the public and include gardens and a woodland walk, a walled kitched garden, lawns and fine views. There is a temporary exhibition of miniature figures by Lilian Lunn. Collections of birds of prey are flown every afternoon (at 3.30pm, weather permitting) on which the grounds are open. Tours of the house are available and commentaries are given. Educational programmes during term time are run from 10am to 2pm exclusively for schools.

Opening Times: May to September inclusive. Sunday, Bank Holiday Monday, Tuesday, Wednesday, Thursday and Friday from 2pm to 5pm.

Booking Requirements: Large parties must book in advance.

Admission Charges: Inclusive charge.

How to get there 8

Address: Leighton Hall, Carnforth, Lancashire LA5 9ST.

Contact: Mrs.S.Reynolds. Tel: Carnforth (0524) 734474 Schools - contact Mr.A.Oswald; (0524) 701353.

Location: Situated between Silverdale, Warton and Yealand Conyers. Approached via the A6 from Kendal to the north, or Lancaster and Carnforth to the south. The Hall is signposted from the A6 at junction 35 with the M6.

Ordnance Survey Grid Reference: SD 494 746.

Parking: Unlimited on the site.

Public Transport: Bus service from Lancaster and Carnforth to Warton or Yealand. Walk approximately 1 mile. Train to Silverdale from Lancaster on the Barrow line, then walk along public footpath across Leighton Moss Reserve to the grounds of the Hall (1 1/2 miles).

Facilities

Catering: Cafeteria with home made teas, ice creams, drinks, etc.

Toilets: Available on the site, no special provision for the disabled but easy access.

Shelter: Yes.

Disabled: Wheelchair ramp. Wheelchairs allowed on Ground Floor and in the grounds.

Amount of Time Taken: Guided tour approximately 45 minutes.

Leaflet/Books/Guides: Yes.

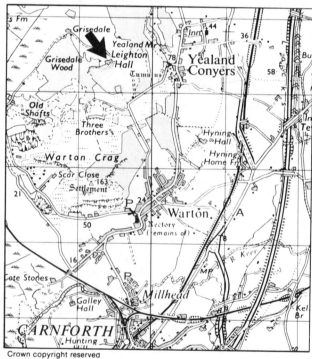

Crown copyright reserved

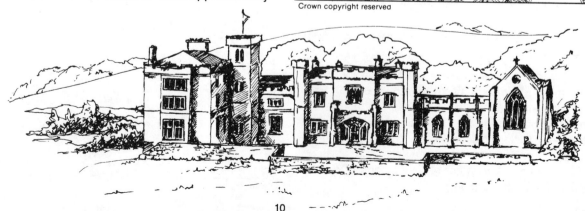

Rufford Old Hall

Early 15th century house built by Sir Thomas Hesketh. Now comprising an original Great Hall of timber construction, a brick wing of 1662 and an intervening section which dates mostly from 1821. The Great Hall contains a magnificent hammer-beam roof and unique medieval carved bog oak screen. Collections of 16th century arms and armour, 17th century furniture, a Beauvais tapestry, a priest's hole and a mid 16th century stone fireplace. Several oil paintings, watercolours and portraits of the Hesketh family can be seen around the walls of the Hall. In the brick wing of the house there are several smaller rooms devoted to a variety of displays. These include the 'Phillip Ashcroft Folk Museum', a reproduction of a village kitchen, a room containing agricultural implements and equipment for making farm produce, a display of tapestries, a display of dresses, dolls and dress accessories, and a room containing a collection of pottery and porcelain. There are no guided tours.

Opening Times: April to end October, everyday except Friday - Hall 1pm-5pm. Gardens, Cafe, Shop 11am-5pm except Friday, closed; Sunday 1pm-5pm but refreshments 2pm-5pm. 1 November-22 December - Hall closed, shop and cafe open 12.30-5pm except Monday and Friday.

Booking Requirements: Parties of 15 or more must be booked in advance. Maximum 50.

Admission Charge: A charge is made for admission. Reduction for parties if prior booking is made.

How to get there 9

Address: Rufford Old Hall, Rufford, Ormskirk L40 1SG.

Contact: The Administrator, Tel: Rufford (0704) 821254.

Location: On the A59 to the north east of the village of Rufford, 7 miles from Ormskirk. When approaching from the south or east leave the M6 at Junction 27 and follow the A5209 to Burscough, then turn north up the A59 to Rufford. From the north travel into Preston and follow signs for Liverpool A59.

Ordnance Survey Grid Reference: SD 463 160.

Parking: Free parking for coaches and cars.

Public Transport: Served by Preston to Liverpool bus, which stops near to Hall. Railway Station at Rufford (not Sunday) 1/2mile, Burscough Bridge 2 1/2miles.

Facilities

Catering: Morning coffee, light lunches, and afternoon teas.

Toilets: Facilities available in the courtyard.

Disabled: Hall not suitable for wheelchairs. Garden and refreshment areas suitable.

Amount of time taken: Half day.

Leaflets/Books/Guides: Rufford Old Hall Official Guide. Various other National Trust Publications.

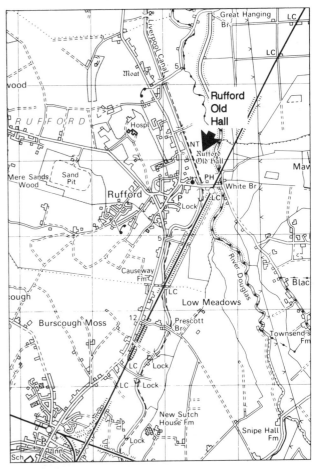

Crown copyright reserved

Samlesbury Hall

The late medieval Hall, a Grade 1 listed builidng, was built by the Southworths during the 14th, 15th and 16th centuries, and was the home of St.John Southworth who was martyred in 1654. Only the great hall and the south wing of 1545 remain but nonetheless it is a very picturesque building. The brick built south wing faces diagonally to the main road but the other side of the wing is of black and white half-timber with the small white quatre-foils making an effective pattern against the black wall. The Hall is now used as a setting for antiques, arts and crafts. An "At Work" series - which changes weekly - features exhibits by local craftsmen. Various exhibitions take place and as there are no guided tours, visitors are free to wander at will throughout the public rooms. The Bowman of Pendle and Samlesbury use an area of pastureland for archery.

Opening Times: Every day except Monday, 11.30am to 4pm winter months, 11.30am to 5pm during British Summer Time. Coach party visits by arrangement during normal opening times but Tuesday to Friday only. The Hall is usually closed from mid-December to mid-January.

Booking Requirements: Party visits must be booked in advance (as much notice as possible - not likely to be available at less than two weeks notice in peak periods).

Admission Charges: A charge is made for admission.

How to get there **10**

Address: Samlesbury Hall, Preston New Road, Samlesbury, Preston PR5 0UP.

Contact: The Administrator, Samlesbury Hall Trust. Tel:Mellor (025481) 2010/2229.

Location: Situated on the A677 Preston New Road approximately half way between Preston and Blackburn. Approaching from Preston the Hall is on the left hand side of the road about a mile past the traffic lights at the junction of A59 and the A677. Approaching from Blackburn the Hall is situated on the right hand side of the A677 just under a mile after the Mellor Brook turn off.

Ordnance Survey Grid Reference: SD 620 304.

Parking: Available at the Hall.

Public Transport: Ribble service 150 Burnley-Preston and X27 Earby-Liverpool, both stopping outside the Hall.

Facilities

Catering: Small cafeteria for light refreshments. Picnicking facilities in the grounds.

Toilets: Inside only and limited.

Shelter: No special wet weather facilities - indoor exhibition facilities only.

Disabled: No special facilities.

Average Length of Time Taken: Approximately half-day.

Group Size: Maximum 100.

Leaflets/Books/Guides: Yes.

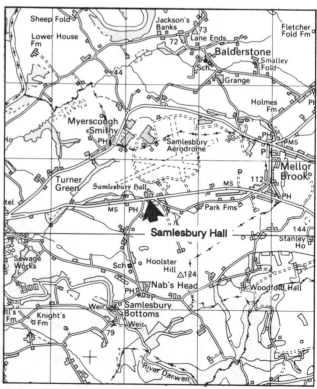

Crown copyright reserved

12

Towneley Hall Art Gallery and Museums

Historic house probably dating from the 14th century, with rooms furnished in period; Art Gallery with collection of 18th and 19th century paintings; Museum with exhibitions and permanent displays; Craft Museum with displays of the main crafts and industries formerly carried out in the local area; Icehouse. Full cafeteria service (light meals and snacks - enquiries for special bookings and menus should be sent to: Mr.&Mrs.Garside, The Old Stables Restaurant, Towneley Park, Burnley BB11 3RQ; telephone (0282) 23441). Picnic tables. Nature centre and woodland trails, and also within Towneley Park and grounds there is an 18 hole golf course, 18 hole pitch and putt, and facilities for tennis and bowls.

Opening Times: Main Hall - Monday to Friday: 10am to 5.30pm. Saturdays: closed throughout the year. Sundays: 12noon to 5pm all year). The Hall is closed on Christmas Day, Boxing Day and New Year's Day. Museum of Local Crafts and Industries - open same hours as Hall in summer and by request on Sundays and weekdays during the winter.

Booking Requirements: Party tours need to be pre-booked, particularly in June and July when it is advisable to book well in advance.

Admission Charges: Free admission to Hall, Museums and Art Gallery.

How to get there 11

Address: Towneley Hall Art Gallery and Museums, Towneley Park, Burnley BB11 3RQ.

Contact: The Curator. Tel:Burnley (0282) 24213.

Location: South east of Burnley approximately 1 1/2 miles from the shopping centre. Entrance to the park is via Lyall Street, off Todmorden Road.

Ordnance Survey Grid Reference: SD 854 309.

Parking: Free parking space for cars and coaches near to the Hall.

Public Transport: Buses:Burnley to Towneley Park, 7 minutes past the hour (Bolton bus) and 36minutes past the hour (Ribble Motors bus).

Facilities

Catering: Yes (see above).

Toilets: Available at the Hall with facilities for the disabled.

Disabled: Toilet facilities. Ramp to Craft and Industries Museum. Although there are stairs in the main Hall, there is wheelchair access to the ground floor and the kitchens. The main exhibitions are usually held on the ground floor level.

Average Length of Time Taken: Guided tours, about 1 to 1 1/2 hours.

Leaflets/Books/Guides: A wide selection is available at the desk.

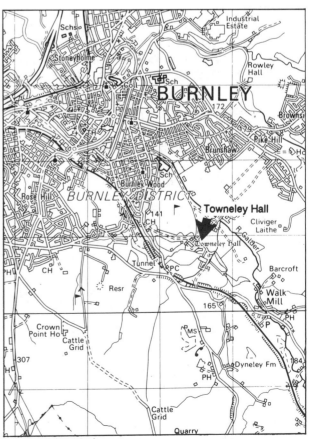

Crown copyright reserved

Turton Tower

The oldest part of Turton Tower is the stone Pele-Tower, built by William Orrell about 1420. In the 16th century two cruck-framed farmhouses were built adjacent to the Tower and in 1596 the Tower was enlarged and a half-timbered entrance wing added. During the Civil War the house was owned by Humphrey Chetham of Manchester, High Sheriff of Lancashire. Restorations were carried out in the 19th century by James Kay who installed the Queen Anne oak panelling and plaster ceilings. The permanent collection includes fine 17th century Lancashire furniture, arms and armour and local history. Temporary exhibitions are held. The house is set in 8 acres of woodland grounds.

Opening Times: May-September Weekdays 10am-12, 1-5pm. Weekdays 1-5pm. October, March, April daily 2-5pm but closed Wednesday and Thursday. November and February Sunday 2-5pm. December, January closed.

Booking Requirements: Party visits must be booked in advance.

Admission Charges: A charge is made for admission.

How to get there 12

Address: Turton Tower, Chapeltown Road, Turton, Bolton BL7 0HG.

Contact: Jocelyn Grigg, Keeper of Turton Tower. Tel:Bolton (0204) 852203.

Location: Turton Tower is situated less than 1/2 mile outside Chapeltown, on the B6391 leading from Chapeltown towards Bromley Cross (1mile). The turning off to Turton Tower is on the right hand side of the road when approaching from Chapeltown.

Ordnance Survey Grid Reference: SD 731 152.

Parking: Car park adjoins. Coaches may park at end of drive.

Public Transport: Bromley Cross railway station on the Bolton to Blackburn line. Bus service from Bolton.

Facilities

Catering: Tea Room.

Toilets: Yes.

Disabled: No facilities for disabled or blind inside the Tower.

Amount of Time Taken: 1hour.

Group Size: Up to 25.

Leaflets/Books/Guides: A Guide to TurtonTower. Postcards etc. available.

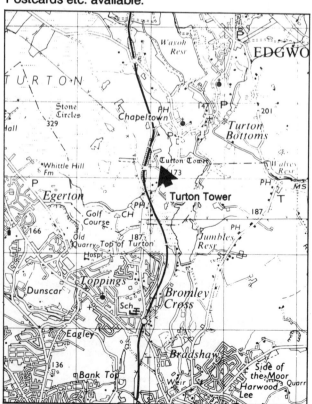

14

Whalley Abbey

Abbey built between 1330 and 1380 is now ruined but with many remaining walls, doors, fireplaces and tombstones, a restored altar and stone pulpit. In 1537 the property was adapted to make an Elizabethan Manor House. A private house until 1923, it is now used as a conference and retreat house for Blackburn Diocese. There is a souvenir and craft shop and a picnic site.

Opening Times: The Abbey ruins and grounds are open from dawn until dusk all year round, and the souvenir and craft shop is open daily from 11.30am to 4.30pm from Easter to end of September.

Booking requirements: It is not necessary to book in advance to view the site but guided tours should be booked in advance.

Admission Charges: A charge is made for admission. Reductions for parties of 12 or more.

How to get there   13

Address: Whalley, Blackburn BB6 9SS.

Contact: The Manager.Tel:Whalley (025482) 2268.

Location: Close to the centre of Whalley approached from Preston along the A59 and Burnley along the A671. Going north along the main street in Whalley (King St.) turn left along Church Lane and after passing a church and school, another left turn leads directly to the Abbey.

Ordnance Survey Grid Reference: SD 730 360.

Parking: Free parking available for cars in the courtyard or outside main gate for coaches.

Facilities

Catering: Sweets, ice-cream and minerals are on sale in the souvenir shop, Easter to September. Meals for parties should be booked well in advance.

Toilets: Available on the site. No disabled toilets.

Shelter: Limited.

Disabled: None, the ruins are not suitable for wheelchairs as there are steps and an uneven surface.

Amount of Time Taken: Up to 2 or 3 hours.

Group size: Any.

Leaflets/Books/Guides: Guide Book and walk round guides.

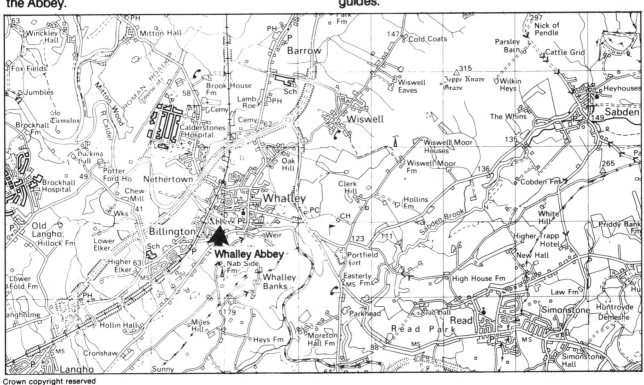

Lancashire has many churches which are well worth a visit. There are two Cathedrals - Blackburn, and St. Peter's Roman Catholic Cathedral, Lancaster. There are historic parish churches in the older towns, such as Lancaster Priory and Ormskirk Parish Church, and there are many churches which reflect the development of the industrial towns. Numerous small country churches have their own attractions; St. Helen's Church at Churchtown, near Garstang, is affectionately known as "The Cathedral of the Fylde". About 200 churches in Lancashire have been Listed as being of special architectural or historic interest.

Lancaster's Priory Church

Museums and Art Galleries

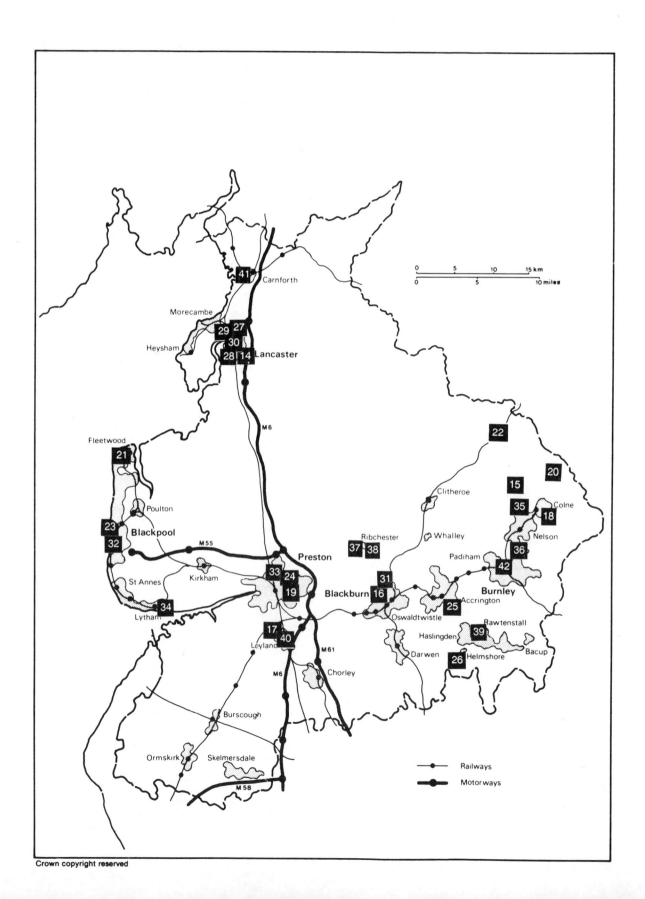

Morecambe

Carnforth

41

Heysham

29 27
30
28 14 Lancaster

M6

Fleetwood

21

Poulton

Clitheroe

22

20

15

35

Colne
18

23

Blackpool

32

M55

St Annes

Kirkham

Ribchester
37 38

Whalley

Nelson

36

Padiham

42

Preston

33 24
19

Burnley

Blackburn
16

31

Accrington
25

34

Lytham

17
40

Leyland

M61

Oswaldtwistle

Rawtenstall
39

Haslingden

Bacup

Darwen

26 Helmshore

M6

Chorley

Burscough

Ormskirk

Skelmersdale

M58

Railways

Motorways

Ashton Memorial and Butterfly House

Dominating from its elevated site in the 38 acre landscaped Williamson Park to the east of Lancaster, the Ashton Memorial has been described as "the grandest monument in England". It was commissioned by the textile and linoleum millionaire James Williamson (later the first Lord Ashton) and completed in 1909 in a High Baroque style to a design by Sir John Belcher. The building now houses an exhibition featuring the Williamson family and their industrial rivals and a multi-projector, stereo sound presentation of aspects of Edwardian life. A gallery affords breathtaking views over the City and surrounding countryside. Located in the former orangery near to the Ashton Memorial, the Butterfly House contains a collection of tropical butterflies. In addition, native species can be viewed in the adjacent Esso English Butterfly Enclosure. Refreshments and other facilities are provided in a period pavilion.

Opening Times: 1 May to 30 September but including Easter - Daily 10am-5pm. 1 October to 30 April- Daily 12 noon-4pm. Butterfly House closed November to January.

Booking Requirements: Advance notice required for coach parties and school groups.

Admission Charges : Admission to Park and Memorial exhibition free. Charge for admission to 'Edwardians' presentation, Viewing Gallery and Butterfly House. School party ticket available. Joint admission ticket available for Ashton Memorial, Butterfly House, Maritime Museum and Cottage Museum.

How to get there 14

Address: The Ashton Memorial, Williamson Park, Lancaster LA1 1UX.

Postal Enquiries to: The Town Clerk, Lancaster City Council, Town Hall, Dalton Square, Lancaster LA1 1JP

Contact: The Supervisor. Tel:Lancaster (0524) 33318.

Location: The Ashton Memorial and Butterfly House are located within Williamson Park which is situated to the immediate east of the City. Access to the Park can be gained from Wyresdale Road and Quernmore Road.

Ordnance Survey Grid Reference: SD 488 614.

Parking: In Williamson Park, access from Wyresdale Road.

Public Transport: Regular bus services run from Lancaster Bus Station, to Wyresdale Road, Park gates.

Facilities

Catering: Refreshments available in adjacent pavilion.

Toilets: Available in adjacent pavilion.

Shelter: Yes and elsewhere within Park.

Disabled: Wheelchair access to Butterfly House and ground floor of Ashton Memorial.

Amount of time taken: 1 1/2- 2 hours.

Group Size: Up to 60.

Leaflets/Books/Guides: Yes.

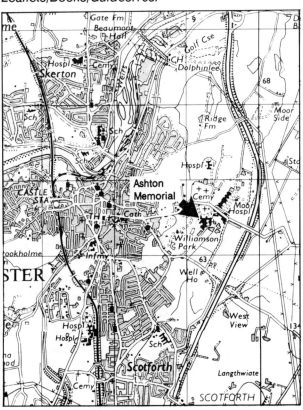

Crown copyright reserved

Bancroft Mill Engine Trust

The Trust is an independent registered charity, formed in 1980 to preserve the industrial heritage of the last working steam mill engine in the area. The objects are to give public exhibitions of the engine and boilerhouse in working order and display other machines, tools and documents relating to the weaving industry in a working museum. Bancroft Shed was built in 1920, the last mill to be built in Barnoldswick, and its 600 bhp cross compound engine by William Roberts & Sons, of Phoenix Foundry, Nelson, drove 1,250 looms until the mill closed in 1978. A recent addition to the attraction is a demonstration of weaving on traditional Lancashire looms including Jaquarette.

Opening Times: Open on steaming days 1pm-5pm and at other times for static viewing by arrangement. Private parties by arrangement. Steaming dates from Easter to October available on request.

Booking Requirements: Prior booking for parties.

Admission Charges: A change is made, with variations between Static Engine Viewing and Steaming Dates.

How to get there 15

Address: Gillians Lane, Barnoldswick, Colne, Lancashire.

Contact: Mr.W.Fisher, 20 School Lane, Earby, Colne, Lancashire BB8 6QB. Telephone:Earby(0282)842214.

Location: From A59 Gisburn to Skipton take B6251 or A56/B6252 for Barnoldswick town centre. Follow B6251, southwards on Manchester Road, for Barrowford and Gillians Lane is 1/2mile on the right.

Ordnance Survey Grid Reference: SD 875 461.

Parking: Free car park.

Public Transport: The Mill is approximately a 10-minute walk from the nearest bus stops on the Skipton and Earby routes. Buses from Colne pass the Mill.

Facilities

Catering: Canteen, Refreshment Room.

Toilets: Available.

Disabled: Provided for.

Average Length of Time Taken: An hour.

*Group Visits:*Maximum number is 50.

*Leaflets/Books/Guides:*Yes.

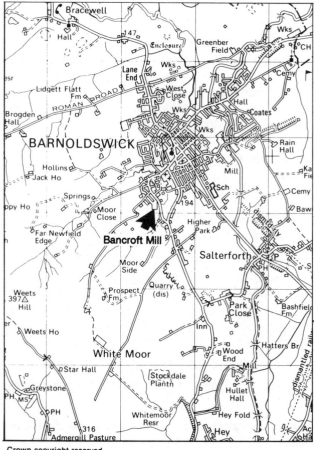

Crown copyright reserved

Blackburn Museum and Art Gallery

Blackburn Museum houses extensive collections relating to local and natural history, Egyptology, ceramics, ethnography and geology. It contains such diverse features as eight works by J.M.W.Turner; one thousand Japanese prints, examples of which are exhibited for a few weeks and then changed round; an Egyptian mummy; the largest British collection of icons outside a national museum; the East Lancashire Regimental Collection and room sets depicting life at the turn of the century. Fine collections of coins, medieval illuminated manuscripts and printed books on show in a new gallery; programme of temporary exhibitions, work of local societies and contemporary artists.

Opening Times: Tuesday - Saturday 10am-5pm.

Admission Charges: None.

How to get there 16

Address: Blackburn Museum and Art Gallery, Museum Street, Blackburn BB1 7AJ.

Contact: The Curator, M.A.E.Millward.

Telephone:Blackburn (0254) 667130.

Location: In Blackburn town centre near the Town Hall.

Ordnance Survey Grid Reference: SD 682 283.

Parking: Visitors should use the car parking facilities in Blackburn town centre.

Public Transport: Good transport system by bus and rail to and from Blackburn town centre.

Facilities

Catering: Town centre facilities.

Toilets: Close by in town centre.

Disabled: Ramped access to ground floor but no access to upper floor. A wheelchair is provided on both floors.

Average Length of Time: An hour or more.

Miscellaneous Information: Loans Service - The Museum can arrange for a display case to be loaned to homes or institutions to house a small display of objects from the Museum's collection which can be changed periodically.

Leaflets/Books/Guides Available: Enterprise sheets (quizzes and trails) - available free of charge for children. Various guides and catalogues.

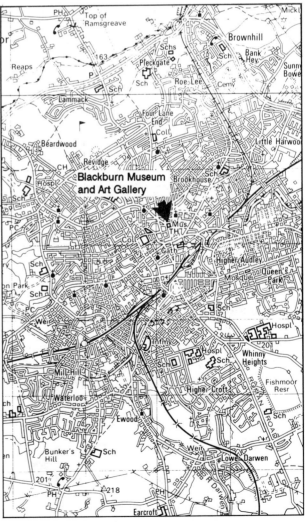

Crown copyright reserved

21

British Commercial Vehicle Museum

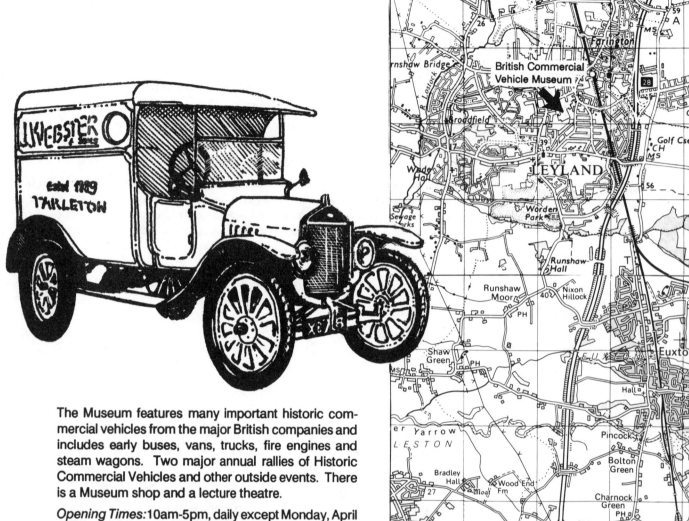

Crown copyright reserved

The Museum features many important historic commercial vehicles from the major British companies and includes early buses, vans, trucks, fire engines and steam wagons. Two major annual rallies of Historic Commercial Vehicles and other outside events. There is a Museum shop and a lecture theatre.

Opening Times: 10am-5pm, daily except Monday, April to September; weekends only October and November. Bank Holidays 10am-5pm.

Admission Charges: A charge is made for admission. Special rates for pre-booked parties.

How to get there **17**

Address: British Commercial Vehicle Museum, King Street, Leyland, Preston PR5 1LE.

Contact: Peter Dawson, Museum Manager. Tel:Leyland (0772) 451011.

Location: King Street (B5254), off Towngate, Leyland. Access from M6 via Junction No.28.

Ordnance Survey Grid Reference: SD 542 223.

Parking: Large car/coach park.

Public Transport: Leyland railway station on the main west coast line is within walking distance of the Museum. There are regular bus services to Leyland from Preston, Chorley and Wigan.

Facilities

Catering: Yes.

Toilets: Yes.

Shelter: The exhibits are housed under cover although from time to time demonstrations will be held in the open air.

Disabled: The Museum is all at ground floor level and is easily accessible to disabled persons in wheelchairs.

Leaflets/Books/Guides Available: Various publications.

British In India Museum

The Museum opened in April 1971 and is housed in a former sweet factory. Attractions include a working model of the Kalka-Simla Railway and the two stations included, those at Kathlighat and Barogh, are correct in detail. There are also photographs showing aspects of the 'British In India' including one of the Calcutta Races in 1912, and a large proportion of the set taken by R.B. Holmes of Peshawa of the Afghan War of 1919. A whole showcase is devoted to Mermanjan, an Afghan Princess who married an English Officer, Captain Thomas Maughan of the East India Company Army, at Kabul in 1849. The effects shown include her clothes, rings, medals and other personal items. A recent donation is a chair covered by a prisoner in Bombay Jail for Anthony Morse when Governor of Bombay. A showcase is devoted to model soldiers of a wide selection of Regiments which are hand made and hand painted in correct detail. There is also a diorama of the Last Stand of the 44th at Gandamak. Other items on show include postage stamps, paintings, medals, military uniforms and postcards.

Opening Times: First Saturday and Sunday in each month, May to September, 2pm-5pm and at other times by arrangement.

Admission Charges : A Charge is made for admission. Special rates for parties of 20 persons or over.

How to get there 18

Address: British in India Museum, Sun Street, Colne, Lancashire BB8 0JJ.

Contact: The Director.

Tel: Nelson (0282) 63129.

Location: Colne is on the main road from Burnley (6 miles) to Keighley (11 miles). Skipton is 12 miles away. The Museum is located in Sun Street, opposite the garage of Seed Ford and behind the shopping centre.

Ordnance Survey Grid Reference : SD 893 401.

Parking: Parking facilities exist around the various side streets and in front of the Museum.

Public Transport: Colne is linked to Burnley and to Preston by direct rail routes and also has direct bus links with Nelson, Skipton, Barnoldswick and Manchester.

Facilities

Catering: There are no formal catering facilities in the Museum. Picnics can be eaten in the small garden

Toilets: Available in the building.

Disabled: The Museum is on one floor and a person in a wheelchair after being lifted up one step could see most of the exhibits.

Amount of Time Taken: Approximately an hour.

Leaflets/Books/Guides Available: Mermanjan - Star of the Evening. Short History of the Indian Army.

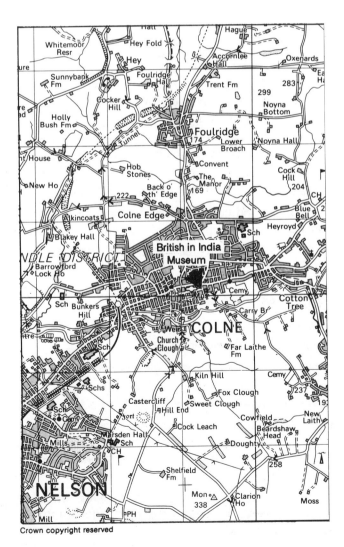

Crown copyright reserved

County and Regimental Museum

This new museum, housed in Preston's former court building, displays items of both military and general interest. The Museum incorporates the regimental collections of the Queen's Lancashire Regiment, the 14th/20th King's Hussars and the Duke of Lancaster's Own Yeomanry. Two galleries tell the story of Lancashire from the Middle Ages, showing the role of the leading landowners, the power of the Church, and the relatively recent work of the County Council. Recreated scenes are used throughout the museum. These include a prisoners' cell from Darwen Police Station, and a First World War trench, complete with sound, light and smell effects! There is also a programme of constantly changing temporary exhibitions.

Opening Times: Open every day (except Thursday and Sunday) 10am-5pm (closed Bank Holidays).

Booking Requirements: Only required for parties over 15 people.

Admission Charges: Free.

How to get there 19

Address: Stanley Street, Preston PR1 4YP. Contact:The Curator. Telephone: Preston (0772) 264075.

Location: Situated on Stanley Street (A6), next to the Prison. From Preston Town Centre the Museum is easily reached on foot, being located at the end of Church Street.

Ordnance Survey Grid Reference: SD 547 296.

Parking: Car and coach parking available. Entrance from A6.

Public Transport: Easily reached on foot from Preston Bus Station.

Facilities

Catering: None.

Toilets: Yes, on the ground floor.

Disabled: Access to most of ground floor only; entrance ramp; special toilet.

Amount of Time Taken: Approximately 1 hour.

Group Size: Parties over 15 are requested to ring the Museum in advance. A separate classroom/meeting room is available, although it must be booked in advance.

Leaflets/Books/Guides Available: A selection of books, postcards, posters and military badges are sold at the Museum shop.

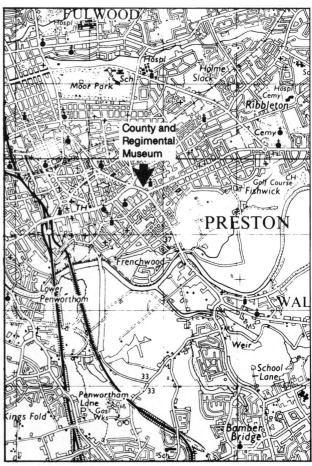

Earby Mines Museum

In 1945 a group of pot holers began to specialise in the derelict lead and other mines in Yorkshire. It was quickly decided to rescue, record and preserve any remains wherever possible. A considerable amount of material was accumulated so that there are now over 600 items. In 1970 the Old Grammar School was offered as a museum and the Yorkshire Dales Lead Mining Museum opened in 1971. (Earby was then in Yorkshire but came within the Lancashire administrative county in 1974). It contains the largest collection of lead mining tools and equipment as used in the Yorkshire Dales, including mine tubs, photographs, plans, mining machinery, personal belongings, and models.

Open: Between last Sunday in March and last Sunday in October on Thursdays 6pm to 9pm and Sundays 2pm to 6pm.

Admission Charges: A charge is made.

Booking Arrangements: Groups during normal hours and by arrangement at other times.

How to get there **20**

Address: The Old Grammar School, School Lane, Earby, Colne.

Contact: Mr.P.Dawson, 41, Stoney Bank Road, Earby, Colne BB8 6RU - Tel.Earby (0282)843210.

Location: Off A56 at the northern end of the town, 4 1/2miles from Colne, 7miles from Skipton.

Ordance Survey Grid Reference: SD 905 469.

Parking: At the front of the Museum and street parking.

Public Transport: Bus route Colne to Skipton.

Facilities

Catering: Picnic table in very attractive grounds. Local facilities.

Toilets: Yes.

Shelter: Indoors.

Disabled: Difficult, an old school building with narrow doors and stairs but every effort made to assist. Advance notice helpful.

Amount of Time Taken: Varies according to interest, casual visitors up to an hour.

Leaflets/Books/Guides Available: Outline leaflet.

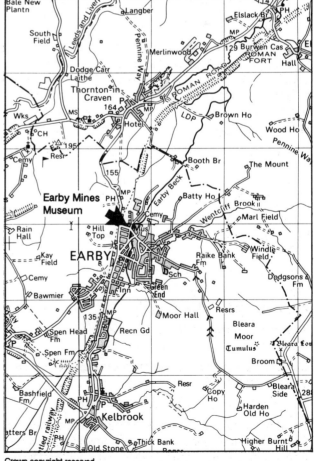

Crown copyright reserved

25

Fleetwood Museum

Fleetwood Museum deals mainly with the fishing industry including methods of trawling, and there is also a section devoted to the history of the town. The Museum has been extended as part of the English Tourist Board's promotion "Maritime England", to provide a permanent display on the sea fisheries of the Lancashire coast. This reflects not only the pre-eminence of Fleetwood as the major west coast deep-sea fishing port but also the diverse fishing activities around the Lancashire coast off Blackpool, in Morecambe Bay, and the estuaries of the Wyre, Lune and Ribble. The Museum occupies the ground floor and basement of the former Whitworth Institute built in 1863 to provide social facilities in the town. The Institute was later, in 1887, given to the town as a Free Library and it continued as the main library until Spring 1988. Displays include a mock trawler bridge, inshore fishing gear arranged in realistic scene settings, trawl doors and nets, as well as more general displays of paintings, drawings, photographs and boat models. For the future, displays are expected to include a reconstructed cottage interior and social aspects of the Fleetwood fishing community. A longer term aim is the restoration and display of the Museum's small inshore fishing boats.

Opening Times: Easter until October open every day except Wednesdays. Monday, Thursday, Saturday, Sunday 2pm-5pm. Tuesday and Friday 10.30am-12.30pm, 1.30pm-5pm.

Booking Requirements: Large parties should ring the Museum or the County Museum Service to give pre-visit warning.

Admission Charges: A charge is made for admission.

How to get there **21**

Address: Fleetwood Museum, Dock Street, Fleetwood.

Contact: Lancashire County Museum Service, Stanley Street, Preston PR1 4YP.

Tel: Preston (0772) 264062 or Fleetwood (03917) 6621.

Location: Situated on Dock Street overlooking the River Wyre, the Museum is only a few minutes walk from the Blackpool tram terminus and Knott End ferry.

Ordnance Survey Grid Reference: SD 339 478.

Parking: No car park at the Museum, but roadside parking is possible and ample parking is adjacent.

Public Transport: Direct bus sevices to Fleetwood from Lancaster, Blackpool and Preston.

Facilities

Catering: None.

Toilets: None.

Shelter: All the exhibits are under cover.

Disabled: No special facilities for the disabled.

Group Sizes: No specific limits, but the Museum is fairly small so groups should not ideally exceed about 40.

Amount of Time Taken: About an hour.

Leaflets/Books/Guides Available: Fleetwood Museum; The Lancashire Sea Fisheries; The Port of Fleetwood; Maritime Lancashire.

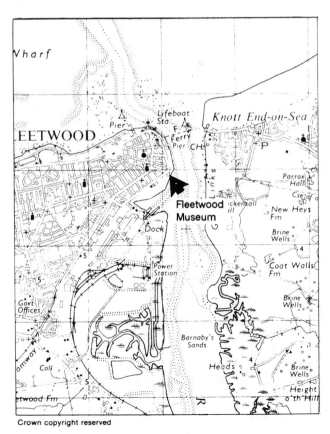

Crown copyright reserved

Steam Museum, Gisburn

The Museum houses a collection of rare steam road vehicles which have been renovated and maintained for exhibition to the public. They include the unique Foster steam wagon, the only known Howard traction engine in Britain, dating from about 1872, a very early Aveling and Porter traction engine, a 1913 Burrell showman's engine, an early Yorkshire steam wagon, and a 115-key modern fairground organ. It should be noted that exhibits attend fetes and rallies and may not all be present on any one day.

Admission Charges: Donation to charity.

Open: The Museum is open to the public from 9am to 5pm daily from March to October inclusive.

Booking Requirements: Coaches by appointment.

How to get there ▪22▪

Address: Steam Museum, Todber Caravan Park, Gisburn, Clitheroe BB7 4JJ.

Proprietors: T.J. & S.Varley.

Contact: Tel:Gisburn (02005)322.

Location: The Museum is situated at the Todber Caravan Park which is accessible from the A682. It is 1 1/2 miles south of the junction of the A682 with the A59 at Gisburn.

Ordnance Survey Grid Reference: SD 835 463.

Parking: Available on the site.

Public Transport: Not accessible by public transport.

Facilities

Toilets: On the site.

Disabled: There are no special facilities for the disabled although the exhibits are at ground level.

Average Length of Stay: About half an hour although visitors may stay for longer periods depending on their level of interest in the exhibits.

Group Size: Up to 50.

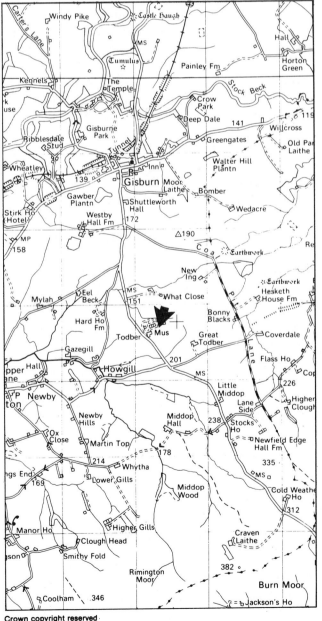

Grundy Art Gallery

Blackpool's municipal Art Gallery, the Grundy, has a fine collection of mainly 19th and 20th century works; British paintings, modern prints; Japanese netsuke and other ivories. Temporary one man and group exhibitions usually on show.

Opening Times: 10am-5pm Monday to Saturday.

Booking Requirements: Pre-booking required for all guided tours. 3 days notice.

Admission Charges: Free.

How to get there 23

Address: Grundy Art Gallery, Queen Street, Blackpool FY1 1PX.

Contact: The Curator, Grundy Art Gallery. Tel:Blackpool (0253) 23977/8.

Location: Near the North Pier and Blackpool North Railway Station in Blackpool town centre. The Gallery is signposted from Talbot Square by the North Pier.

Ordnance Survey Grid Reference: SD 308 366.

Parking: Car park (pay) next to Art Gallery.

Public Transport: Blackpool is well served with bus routes both locally and to other parts of the country. The Art Gallery is also within a few hundred yards of Blackpool North Station.

Facilities

Catering: Town centre facilities.

Toilets: Town centre facilities.

Disabled: Special entrance available.

Average Length of Time Taken: About an hour unless specialised study.

Group Size: Up to 20.

Leaflet/Books/Guides Available: Forthcoming Events leaflets (free).

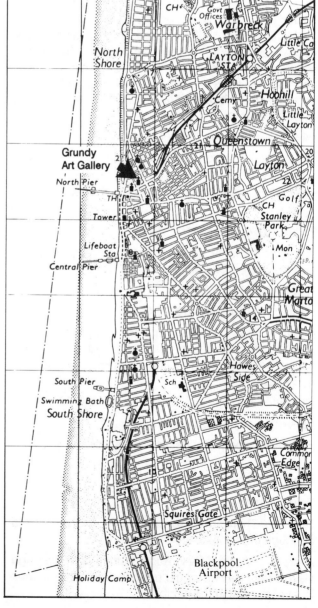

Crown copyright reserved

28

Harris Museum and Art Gallery

The Harris' lively exhibition programme shows exciting work by contemporary artists and crafts people of national and international repute, as well as new talent. The exhibitions are supported by talks, events and activities. There are fine collections of British 19th and 20th century paintings and sculptures and extensive collections of decorative art, costume and textiles, ceramics and glass. "Story of Preston" traces the development of the town over 12,000 years. Striking features are a 17th century market stall, and a reconstructed corner shop and terraced house. The Social History Gallery houses temporary exhibitions of local and historical interest which bring the story up to the present.

Opening Times: Monday to Saturday 10am-5pm.

Booking Requirements: It is necessary to book in advance for guided tours as the guides are voluntary. At least one week's notice is required.

Admission Charges: None.

How to get there

Address: Harris Museum and Art Gallery, Market Square, Preston PR1 2PP.

Contact: Museum and Art Officer.
Tel:Preston (0772) 58248.

Location: The Harris Museum and Art Gallery is situated in Preston town centre, near the Guild Hall and is signposted from the main shopping streets.

Ordnance Survey Grid Reference: SD 541 296.

Parking: The Museum has no car park of its own, but there are multi storey and ground level car parks in the town centre.

Public Transport: Good transport system by bus and rail to and from Preston town centre. Both the bus and railway stations are within easy walking distance.

Facilities

Catering: Refreshments available Monday-Saturday, 10.45am-4pm.

Toilets: There are no toilet facilities in the Museum, but public toilets are situated at the Covered Market nearby and at Preston Bus Station.

Disabled: There is a lift in the Museum and a special entrance for wheelchairs in Lancaster Road.

Amount of Time Taken: One or two hours.

Leaflets/Books/Guides Available: There is an extensive range of publications.

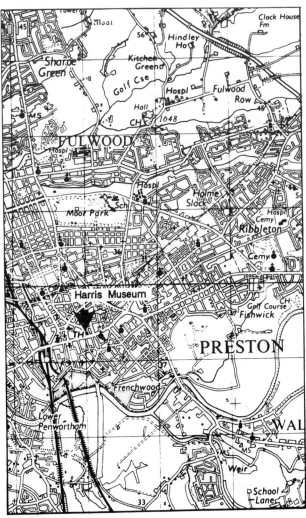

Crown copyright reserved

Haworth Art Gallery

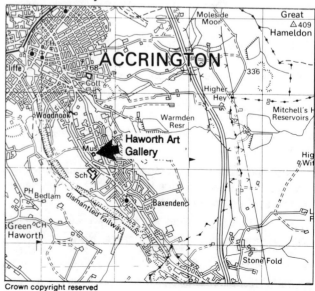

Fine building erected in 1909 for the Haworth family - left to Accrington in 1920 to be the town's Art Gallery. The building is still in its original state, and the series of rooms allow for many exhibitions to run at the same time. Exhibitions are changed monthly. There is a small concert room, where concerts are held regularly. Besides travelling exhibitions there is a good permanent collection which includes work by Vernet, Herring Senior, Stark, Birkett-Foster, Cox and many other painters, but the main attraction is the Tiffany Glass collection, which is the finest in Europe and one of the finest in the world. It is attractively displayed and is on permanent exhibition. The Gallery is situated in a superb semi-wild Park with excellent views across a valley. The Park covers 13 1/2 acres and contains a number of interesting specimens of plant life. There is a first class Nature Trail booklet by Charles Gidman and this embraces both the Park and the Gallery. The Curator is prepared to give talks on the Gallery, etc., and is available most afternoons. He can also give guided tours. There is a Brass Rubbing Centre where prices vary from 10p-£1.10 depending on sizes, etc. Materials and instruction are given.

Opening Times: 2pm-5pm Monday to Thursday and Saturday and Sunday (closed Friday). The Gallery is closed Christmas Day, Boxing Day, New Year's Day and Good Friday.

Booking Requirements: Guided tours and special booking may be made for parties, clubs and organisations during mornings and evenings. Tea, coffee and biscuits can be made available for a small fee.

Admission Charges: Free.

How to get there 25

Address: Haworth Art Gallery, Haworth Park, Manchester Road, Accrington.

Contact: The Curator (for morning and evening parties).
Tel: Accrington (0254) 33782.

Location: Haworth Park is situated on Manchester Road, which is the road from Accrington-Baxenden/Manchester. a)From Accrington town centre follow the A680 Manchester Road towards Haslingden, passing the police and fire stations and Oak Hill Park on the right. Turn right onto Harcourt Road and follow the Gallery signs. b)If coming from Rossendale, Bury, or Manchester direction use the M66 and follow the Accrington signs, come off at Rising Bridge when the road becomes Manchester Road and follow the Accrington signs. Using Holland's Pie Works on the left as a land mark, the next landmark, Alma Inn is also on the left followed soon after by a left turn into Newton Drive and then follow the Gallery signs.

Ordnance Survey Grid Reference: SD 768 272.

Parking: Yes, at Gallery.

Public Transport: Good local bus and train routes to all surrounding areas.

Facilities

Catering: There is a picnic area and many large lawns available for picnicking. There are no catering facilities, but the Gallery has a drink vending machine.

Toilets: Yes including facilities for the disabled.

Disabled: The disabled can look around the ground floor with ease and the doors are wide enough to take wheelchairs but there is no lift to the upper floor. The Curator is prepared to take blind people round and describe the exhibits.

Group Size: No limits.

Average Amount of Time Taken: Approximately a half day trip.

Miscellaneous: Picture lending library - fine collection of framed reproductions - nearly 300 pictures in all. There is a modest fee for the loan of the pictures, which can be borrowed for three months at a time.

Leaflets/Books/Guides Available: Full coloured catalogue which covers the building, permanent collection, Tiffany Glass and Park, Postcards of the Tiffany Glass, Nature Trail guide by Charles Gidman covering the Park and Gallery.

Crown copyright reserved

Helmshore Textile Museums

The working atmosphere of an early Lancashire cotton mill can still be experienced at Helmshore, where aspects of the County's textile heritage are preserved on two adjoining mill sites. A late 18th century woollen fulling mill, Higher Mill, complete with its magnificent working water wheel and fulling stocks, also houses a unique collection of early textile carding and spinning machines. The collection includes an improved Hargreaves spinning jenny and Arkwright's water frame. The adjacent 19th century Whitakers Mill contains a display which outlines Lancashire's historical involvement with wool, flax and cotton textiles. An upper floor preserves the working environment of a cotton spinning mill. Working demonstrations include the 1903 Taylor Lang mules, carding engines and a Derby doubler.

Opening Times: Sundays Easter to October 31: 11am-5pm. November to Easter:2pm-5pm. Weekdays Easter to June 30 and October:2pm-5pm. July to September 30:12noon-5pm. Saturday July to September 30:2pm-5pm. Bank Holiday Weekends open but closed Christmas Day, Boxing Day, New Year's Day.

Booking Requirements: Guided Tours and School Parties. Coach parties welcomed.

Group Size: Guided tours maximum of 40. School parties of up to 60 children.

Admission Charges: A single charge is made for admission to both museums. There is a separate charge for guided tours. Reduction for bookings paid in advance.

How to get there 26

Address: Holcombe Road, Helmshore, Rossendale, Lancashire BB4 4NP.

Contact: Museum Manager.
Tel:Rossendale (0706) 226459.

Location: One mile south of Haslingden on the B6235.

Ordnance Survey Grid Reference: SD 779 212.

Parking: Free car/coach park adjacent to the Museum.

Public Transport: The Museum is difficult to reach by public transport, but is served locally by the Haslingden via Helmshore circular bus route. On Sundays Easter to October a bus service links the Museum with the East Lancashire Railway at Ramsbottom.

Facilities

Catering: Picnic tables are available in the car park. Cafeteria serving light refreshments.

Toilets: Includes a toilet for the disabled.

Disabled: The mills can be visited quite easily by people in wheelchairs. Only the upper floors of Higher Mill are inaccessible.

Average Length of Time Taken: Casual visits approximately 1-1 1/2hours. Guided tours approximately 2 hours.

Leaflets/Books/Guides Available: Guide Leaflets, Postcards and various booklets.

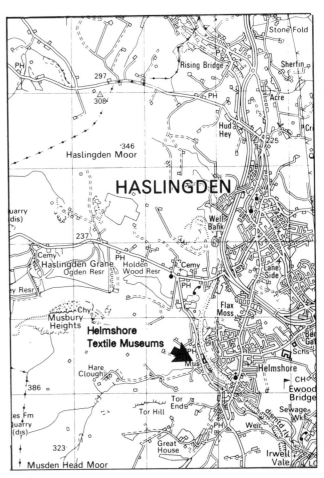

Crown copyright reserved

31

Judges' Lodgings Museum

A 17th century town house in the centre of Lancaster, developed as a Museum of Lancashire Childhood and a Museum of Gillow Furniture. The Childhood displays on the top floor include dolls from the Barry Elder doll collection, once housed at Carr House, Bretherton, and period rooms depicting Victorian childhood in the County. The ground and first floors of the building have been used to illustrate the history of the house and to display, in period settings, furniture made by the firm of Gillow of Lancaster. There is a souvenir shop selling toys, books and postcards.

Opening Times: From Good Friday to the end of October: April: Monday-Friday 2pm-5pm; May and June: Monday-Saturday 2pm-5pm; July, August and September: Monday-Friday 10am-1pm, 2pm-5pm, Saturday 2pm-5pm; Bank Holiday Weekends: Saturday, Sunday and Monday 2pm-5pm.

Admission Charges: A charge is made for admission.

How to get there 27

Address: Judges' Lodgings, Church Street, Lancaster LA1 1YS.

Contact: The Keeper. Telephone:Lancaster (0524) 32808.

Location: The Museum is situated in Lancaster city centre, near to the Castle and Priory Church (a location map can be obtained from the Museum on request).

Ordnance Survey Grid Reference: SD 476 618.

Car and Coach Parking: Coaches may stop briefly outside the Judges' Lodgings to allow passengers off and on. Parking facilities for coaches and cars are available in the city centre, and are marked on the Museum's location map.

Public Transport: There is a good public transport service and the Museum is within walking distance of the railway and bus stations.

Facilities

Food and Drink: A small coffee bar (maximum capacity 24) offering drinks and biscuits will be open at certain times during Museum hours.

Toilets: Public toilet facilities opposite.

Disabled: No special facilities but every effort will be made to assist an individual in a wheelchair on and between all floors. Notice of visit is requested. Not suitable for groups of disabled persons in wheelchairs.

Average Length of Stay: Dependent on individual interest but allow a minimum of 3/4hour.

Group Size: Maximum 50 adults. Children, accompanied by adults, maximum 40.

Leaflets/Books/Guides Available: Yes, including History of Gillow of Lancaster; Dolls Leaflet; History of the House.

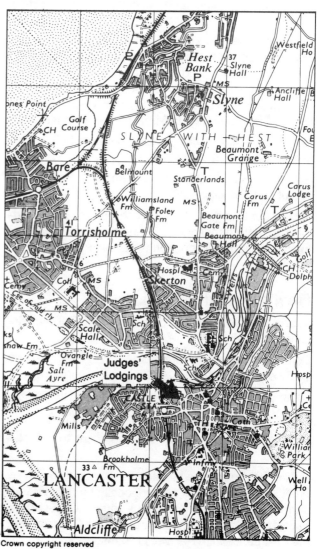

Crown copyright reserved

Lancaster City Museum

The Museum chiefly illustrates the development of local life from the earliest times to the present day. Inscribed stones, including a milestone from Caton, provide significant knowledge of Roman Lancaster, and Saxon cross fragments, dug-out boats, and remains from Cockersands Abbey survive from the Middle Ages. A series of relief maps and watercolour paintings describe the changing appearance of the city itself and much of the character of old Lancaster is recorded in a series of photographs from the turn of the century. Of particular interest are weights and measures, clocks, firearms, ship models, railway and canal items, local pottery, and exhibits of furniture making. An extensive collection (with which the Museum has been associated since 1929) of the King's Own Regiment includes early uniforms, medals and photographs. Temporary exhibitions of decorative art are also feature.

Admission Charges: None.

Opening Times: All year except ChristmasDay/New Year. Monday-Friday 10am-5pm, Saturday 10am-3pm.

Booking Requirements: Groups by prior arrangement and outside normal hours can be considered.

Facilities

Catering: None.

Toilets: None in the Museum but there are some within a few minutes walk.

*Disabled:*There are no lifts for the disabled but there is access to the ground floor.

Average Length of Time Taken: General visits 3/4 to 1 1/2hour.

Miscellaneous: Guided Walks - From the third Wednesday in July to the third Wednesday in September guided walks are available around the principal features of interest in and around the historic city centre. Walks commence from the museum at 2pm on each of the above Wednesdays and there is no charge.

Leaflet/Books/Guides Available: Yes. An extensive selection.

How to get there 28

Address: City Museum, Market Square, Lancaster LA1 1HT.

Contact: Curator (A.J.White, MA, FMA, FSA) Tel:Lancaster (0524) 64637.

Location: The Museum is in the Market Square in the pedestrianised City centre and is signposted from the city centre.

Ordnance Survey Grid Reference: SD 476 618.

Parking: The Museum has no car park of its own and visitors should use the car parking facilities in Lancaster. A multi-storey car park is nearby in Lower Church Street/Great John Street.

Public Transport: The railway and bus stations are within 5 minutes walk.

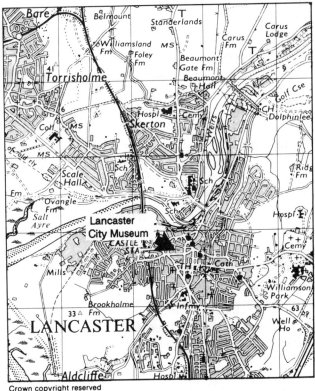

Crown copyright reserved

Lancaster Cottage Museum and Music Room

The Cottage Museum is part of a larger house built or rebuilt in 1739 and originally was a house with a shop on the left-hand side. In about 1825-30 the house was divided into two. The property fell into disrepair but between 1976 and 1978 this and other buildings on the corner facing the Castle were all restored. The right-hand half is now a private house but the left-hand was returned to approximately its 1825 condition and furnished as an artisan's cottage. The Music Room was probably built 1730-40 originally as a garden house for the Marton family. It was rescued from dereliction by the Landmark Trust and a lengthy restoration was completed in 1975. The whimsical exterior hides possibly the finest and most exuberant baroque plasterwork interior in the north west. Thought to be the work of the Italian master craftsman Vassali it took 6,000 man-hours to restore. Performances of period music are occasionally held.

Open: Cottage Museum Easter then mid May - end September, daily 2pm - 4pm. Music Room March to October Saturday 11am - 2pm and other times by arrangements.

Booking Requirements: Group visits book in advance.

Admission Charges: Charge at the Cottage Museum, Music Room free.

How to get there 29

Address: The Cottage Museum, Castle Hill, Lancaster. The Music Room, Sun Street, Lancaster.

Contact: Andrew White, Curator, City Museum, Market Square, Lancaster LA1 1HT.
Tel:Lancaster (0524) 64637.
David Wright, Honorary Administrator, The Music Room, c/o 82 Dallas Road, Lancaster LA1 1TW.
Tel:Lancaster (0524) 39741 Ext.333 and 60658.

Location: Cottage Museum is opposite the Castle. The Music Room is quite close with access to Sun Street from Church Street and Market Street.

Ordnance Survey Grid References: SD 475 619 and SD 475 618.

Parking: City centre car parks.

Public Transport: Rail and bus stations are within walking distance.

Facilities

Catering: City centre facilities.

Toilets: Public toilets nearby.

Shelter: Yes.

Disabled: There are no special facilities. The Cottage Museum is unsuitable for wheelchairs and access to The Music Room is up a steep flight of stairs.

Amount of Time Taken: Cottage Museum about 1/2 hour; Music Room varies, lengthy if there is a special interest in interior decoration.

Group Size: Cottage Museum maximum 20, Music Room 35.

Leaflets/Books/Guides: Yes.

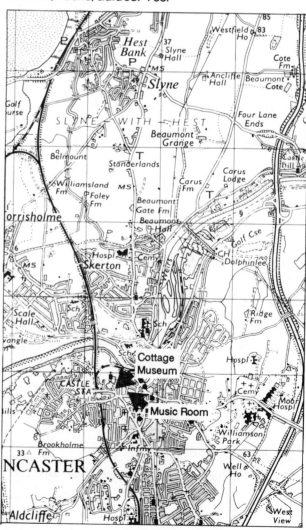

Lancaster Maritime Museum

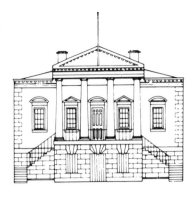

The Museum is concerned with the story of the maritime history and environment of Lancaster and district from the earliest times. The magnificent restored Custom House of 1764 concentrates on the prosperous 18th century trade with the West Indies and North America, and the important fishing industry of Morecambe Bay. Full-size examples of local fishing boats, a reconstructed fisherman's cottage scene and 'sound points' where recollections of life in the fishing community can be heard, all illustrate the nature of the industry. In the extension, opened in 1987 in the adjoining 18th century port warehouse, similar reconstructions, audio points and even smells help recreate local history. A walk-in replica section of the fast canal packet boat "Waterwitch" is the centre-piece of a display on the Lancaster Canal; and visitors can pass through a tubular steel mock-up of a gas rig surrounded by items of production machinery describing the extraction of natural gas in Morecambe Bay. Amongst many other displays are the development of local tourism and an examination of the ecology of the Bay.

Opening Times: Daily 11am-5pm April-October, 2pm-5pm November-March. Closed Christmas and New Year.

Booking Requirements: Groups preferably by prior arrangement. Times outside normal hours will be considered.

Admission Charges: November-March: free. April-October: a charge is made for admission.

How to get there 30

Address: Custom House, St.George's Quay, Lancaster LA1 1RB.

Contact: Curator (A.J.White, MA, FMA, FSA) Telephone:Lancaster (0524) 64637

Location: The Museum is housed in the old porticoed Custom House on Lancaster Quayside and is signposted from the City centre.

Ordnance Survey Grid Reference: SD 473 623.

Parking: There is ample parking to the rear of the Museum and on Quayside. Access to the multi-storey car park is at the end of the Quay, from Damside Street.

Public Transport: Both the bus and railway stations are a brief walk from the Museum.

Facilities

Catering: Small cafe.

Toilets: Provided, suitable for disabled persons.

Disabled: Access suitable for disabled.

Amount of Time Taken: Generally 1-1 1/2 hours.

Group Size: No maximum number. Approximately 30 if a guided tour required.

Leaflets/Books/Guides Available: Many local maritime history publications.

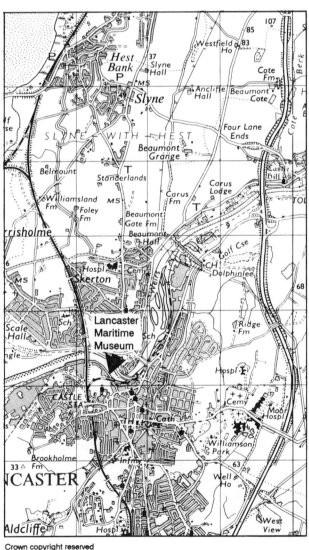

Lewis Textile Museum

Thomas Boyes Lewis believed that Blackburn would benefit from having a museum dedicated to the history of the textile industry and presented this building, with its collection, to the town in 1937. The ground floor is arranged as a series of rooms showing the different textile machines of the Industrial Revolution, from the spinning wheel to the 19th century Lancashire Loom and include Kay's flying shuttle, Hargreave's spinning jenny, Arkwright's water frame and Crompton's 'mule'. Groups, who should book in advance, can see some of the machinery in operation. On the upper floor of the Museum there is a gallery for temporary exhibitions of paintings, sculptures and photographs by local artists and societies.

Opening Times: Open 10am-5pm Tuesday to Saturday, all year. Closed Sunday and Monday, Bank Holidays.

Booking Requirements: In advance for guided tour.

Admission Charges: Free.

How to get there 31

Address: Lewis Textile Museum, Exchange Street, Blackburn.
Contact: The Curator.
Telephone: Blackburn (0254) 667130.
Location: In the centre of Blackburn opposite the Town Hall and near to Blackburn Museum and Art Gallery.
Ordnance Survey Grid Reference: SD 681 283.
Parking: Available nearby on shopping centre car park (pay). Limited free street car parking in the vicinity.
Public Transport: The Museum is within fairly easy walking distance of Blackburn bus station and railway station.

Facilities

Catering: No catering facilities, but public houses and cafes nearby in the town centre.
Toilets: No toilet facilities on the premises but there are public toilets including disabled facilities about 100 yards away.
Disabled: Access for the disabled is possible but not easy.

Average Length of Time Taken: Pre-booked guided tours show machines operating and the duration is up to 1 1/2 hours.

Group Sizes: Ideally should not be in excess of 20 per group but larger can be split up.

Leaflets/Books/Guides Available: Various publications.

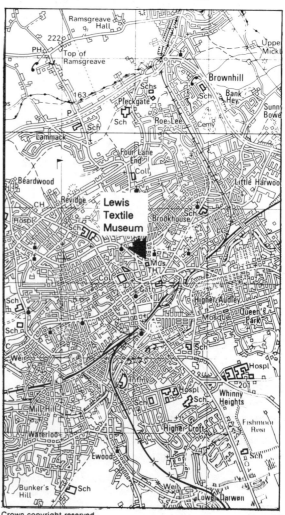

Crown copyright reserved

Louis Tussaud's Waxworks

Many displays of wax models and scenes containing wax figures, Hall of tableaux featuring "James Bond - 007", "Silent Movies", "Pop Stars". Grand Hall containing models of members of royal families, politicians, film stars, etc. Chamber of Horrors with famous murderers and such delights at Frankenstein, Dracula and the "Phantom of the Opera" tableaux. There is an anatomy exhibition which is strictly reserved for adults only. There are animated educational tableaux in some sections.

Opening Times: Seven days per week, Saturday before Good Friday until the end of October. Open from 10am until 5pm (early season) and until 10pm (peak season). Open winter weekends.

Booking Requirements: No advance booking required to view the exhibition but guided tours and lectures are available only on application and are subject to business.

Admission Charges: A charge is made for admission. Disabled persons admitted free of charge each Friday.

How to get there 32

Address: Louis Tussaud's Waxworks (Blackpool) Ltd., 87/89 Central Promenade, Blackpool FY1 5AA.

Contact: General Manager. Tel: Blackpool (0253) 25953.

Location: On the Central Promenade in Blackpool, between the Tower and the Pleasure Beach, almost opposite the Central Pier entrance. Regular buses from the bus station and Blackpool North railway station.

Ordnance Survey Grid Reference: SD 306 354.

Car and Coaching Parking: A car park is situated behind the premises (Bonny Street) and a coach park on Central Drive.

Facilities

Catering: No cafe but food and drink vending machines are available.

Toilets: Available on the 2nd and 3rd floors, but no special provision for the disabled.

Disabled: No special disabled facilities, although the disabled and handicapped are welcomed. It must be noted that there is no public lift for wheelchairs between the floors. Group visitors by disabled persons can only be made by prior written application.

Average Length of Stay: Between 1 and 2 hours.

Group Size: No limit.

Leaflets/Books/Guides Available: Louis Tussaud's Waxworks Guide, Postcards of waxworks.

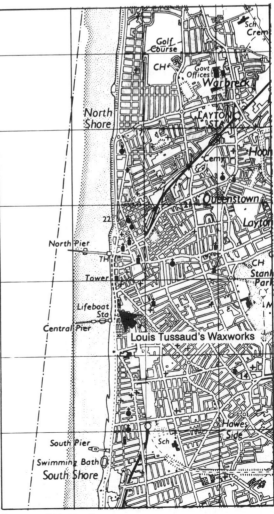

The Loyal Regiment

Fulwood Barracks, Preston, houses the regimental museum of the 47th and 81st, The Loyal Regiment (North Lancashire). Of the many fascinating exhibits the most famous is the silver-mounted Maida Tortoise associated with the battle of Maida (1806) when a small British force landed in southern Italy and defeated Napoleon's hitherto invincible veterans. The 47th became known as "Wolfe's Own" and there are exhibits associated with the General. A set of six Russian drums and a double headed eagle are souvenirs from the Crimean War and there are many items commemorating the Defence of Kimberley, a unique battle honour of the 1st Battalion The Loyals for its lone defence of the diamond town. Swords, uniforms, badges and buttons are amongst many other trophies of peace and war. The Loyal Regiment is now absorbed into the Queen's Lancashire Regiment, see the County and Regimental Museum entry.

Open: Tuesday and Thursday, 9.15am-12.15pm, 2.15pm-4.15pm. Other times by arrangement for 5 or more.

Booking Requirements: Parties of 5 or over should make advance arrangements.

Admission Charges: None. Donations are welcomed.

How to get there 33

Address: The Loyal Regiment (NL) Museum, Fulwood Barracks, Preston PR2 4AA

Contact: Major N.J.Perkins. Tel:Preston (0772) 716543 Ext.2362.

Location: On B6242, off A6 1 1/2 miles south of M6/M55 interchange. North of A5085, Blackpool Road, 1/4 mile north of Preston North End football ground.

Ordnance Survey Grid Reference: SD 548 315.

Parking: Not within the Barracks. Street parking opposite.

Public Transport: Bus services from the town centre.

Facilities

Catering: Adjacent public houses.

Toilets: Yes.

Shelter: Indoors.

Disabled: Welcomed, but no special provision for wheelchairs.

Amount of Time Taken: Depends on degree of interest, casual visitor 30 minutes.

Group Size: Maximum 15 at any one time.

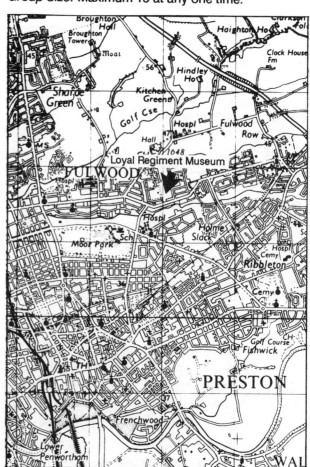

Lytham Motive Power Museum

A selection of rolling stock is on display which includes a standard gauge Class G locomotive built in 1887 which was finally operated by British Rail No.68095. This engine is now in the passenger livery of the North British Railway. Other locomotives are Pax, a former works shunter at Vulcan Foundry; Penicuick, Ribblesdale No.3, and Hotto. Exhibits are occasionally loaned to other museums. The Lytham Creek Railway is of 10 3/4 inches Gauge. There are a number of exhibits of railway miscellany as well as several road vehicles on display. These include a Burrell steam roller of 1913. Small souvenir shop selling jigsaws, books, slides, car stickers, pictures of engines. Miniature train engine display and engine which children can climb on and explore.

Booking Requirements: Group visits should be arranged at least a few days before intended visit.

Admission Charges: A charge is made for admission.

Opening Times: 11am until 4pm (every day except Monday, Friday and Saturday but open on Bank Holiday Mondays.

How to get there 34

Address: Lytham Motive Power Museum, Dock Road, Lytham.

Contact: Tel:Lytham (0253) 733122.

Location: Situated off the main Preston Road leading into Lytham from the east. Entering Lytham via Preston Road take the left hand turn at the traffic lights by the post office, and go down Dock Road in the Lytham Creek area. The Museum is then situated towards the end of the road on the right hand side.

Ordnance Survey Grid Reference: SD 382 275.

Parking: No car park but parking available by roadside near the Museum.

Public Transport: Lytham town centre is in fairly easy walking distance and has good bus and train links with St.Annes, Blackpool and Preston.

Facilities

Catering: No formal picnicking facilities but cans of drink can often be purchased at the small souvenir shop.

Toilets: Not generally open to the public.

Shelter: Most of the exhibits under cover.

Disabled: No special facilities for the disabled.

Average Length of Time Taken: Under an hour.

Leaflets/Books/Guides Available: Lytham Creek Railway and Motive Power Museum - Stock List. Several publications on the history of railways.

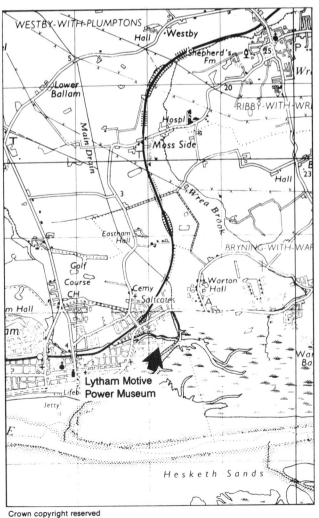

Pendle Heritage Centre

Park Hill is an historic farmhouse dating from the 17th/18th century and provides the ideal setting for a study of the region's vernacular architectural and rural heritage. The house and surrounding farm buildings are being restored to illustrate the building phases of a Lancashire house and the changes in domestic life down the ages. There is an 18th century walled garden, a 17th century cruck-frame barn, Barrowford Toll-House, audio visual presentations and farming displays. The Centre has rooms available throughout the year for lectures and meetings. Colne Heritage Centre in the Grammar School at Colne is an outpost; it opens May to September Saturday 10-4 and Wednesday 2-4.30pm and stages changing exhibitions.

Opening Times: Exhibitions - Tuesday, Wednesday, Thursday, Saturday, Sunday, Bank Holiday Mondays 2-4.30pm from Easter to last Sunday in November. Enquiries - weekdays 9am - 5pm all year.

How to get there 35

Address: Pendle Heritage Centre, Park Hill, Barrowford, Nelson BB9 6JQ.

Contact: Mr.E.M.J.Miller. Tel:Nelson(0282)695366.

Location: Situated at Park Hill, Barrowford. Approximately 5miles from Burnley town centre. Follow A682 out of Nelson through Barrowford. The Centre is situated on the right across the bridge, where B6247 joins the main road.

Ordnance Survey Grid Reference: SD 683 398.

Parking: Free car park opposite the Centre, not large enough for coaches but it is possible for them to park on the road adjacent to the Centre. Mini buses can be accommodated on the car park.

Public Transport: Pendle and Burnley JTC/Ribble Services 60 and 61 from Burnley and Nelson - alight at "Park Gates".

Facilities

Catering: Tea room, picnic sites.

Toilets: Available at the Centre.

Shelter: Guided tours are inside the house, but can be combined with routed walks from the Centre.

Disabled: Every assistance offered to individuals; advance telephone call appreciated.

Average Length of Time Taken: About 1 1/2 hours.

Group Size: 60 maximum for guided tours and refreshments.

Leaflets/Books/Guides Available: Pendle Heritage Centre - information leaflet. Pendle Heritage Centre, newsletters. Variety of other books, leaflets, magazines and guides to the area.

Crown copyright reserved

Queen Street Mill

Take a step back in time at the Queen Street Mill. This is an authentic example of a 19th century weaving shed, and was the country's last steam powered mill, remaining virtually unchanged until its closure in 1982. Now re-opened as Britain's only working steam powered weaving mill museum, there is the magnificent original 500hp steam driven mill engine "PEACE" which powers about 200 authentic Lancashire looms and other machinery for weaving cloth which is then sold in the shop. It is also made up into top quality goods including traditional Union Shirts, as worn by the men weavers but which are now regarded as high fashion garments for both sexes. Staff on duty at weekends wear authentic costume. There are educational facilities, exhibitions and a traditional mill shop.

Opening Times: Thursday, Friday, Saturday, Sunday and Bank Holiday Mondays, 10.30am-4.30pm.

Booking Requirements: Necessary for 30 plus groups.

Admission Charges: A charge is made for admission.

How to get there 36

Address: Harle Syke, Burnley BB10 2HX.

Contact: Mrs. Anna Benson.
Tel:Burnley (0282) 412555.

Location: About 2 miles north east of Burnley town centre to the east of A56 on the Briercliffe Road. Turn right (heading Burnley to Briercliffe) into Queen Street after the Post Office. From Junction10 on M65 follow A56 for Burnley, turning left onto A6114 and then left after 3/4mile onto Briercliffe Road.

Parking: Ample.

Public Transport: Local bus service from Burnley bus station.

Ordnance Survey Grid Reference: SD 868 352

Facilities

Catering: Cafe serving drinks and snacks.

Toilets: Yes.

Shelter: Under cover.

Disabled: The mill is on ground floor level except for the engine. Disabled toilet under construction.

Amount of Time Taken: 45 minutes.

Group Size: Over 30 book in advance.

Leaflets/Books/Guides Available: Yes.

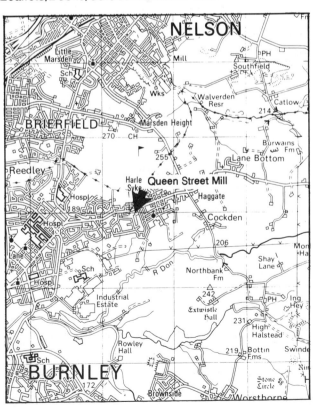

Crown copyright reserved

Ribchester Museum of Childhood

The Museum consists of a private collection of toys, models, dolls, 54 doll's houses, miniatures, curios, etc. with special attractions of a 20-piece working model fairground, General Tom Thumb memorabilia and Professor Tomlim's Flea Circus. There are tea-rooms, an exhibition room, small stage for occasional puppet and Punch and Judy shows and next door there is a traditional toy shop, selling gifts, toys, dolls and collectors' items.

Opening Times: 11am to 5pm all year round Tuesday to Sunday, closed Mondays but open Bank Holidays.

Booking Requirements: Telephone for details.

Admission Charges: A charge is made for admission.

How to get there 37

Address: Church Street, Ribchester, Lancashire PR3 3YE.

Contact: David and Ankie Wild.

Telephone: Ribchester (025484) 520.

Location: In the centre of Ribchester village, 15 minutes from exit 31 on M6.

Ordnance Survey Grid Reference: SD 650 352.

Parking: Large public free car park nearby.

Public Transport: Local bus service.

Facilities

Catering: Tea and coffee room.

Toilets: Toilet rooms for the public.

Shelter: All exhibits indoors.

Disabled: Wide staircase to first floor. No lift.

Amount of time taken: About 1 hour.

Group Size: Up to 50.

Leaflets/Books/Guides Available: Yes, including School Questionnaire.

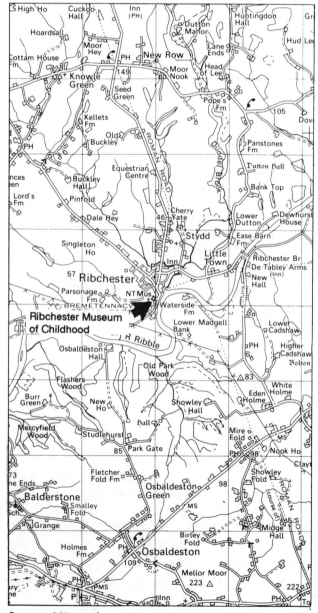

Ribchester Museum of Roman Antiquities

Independent Museum of Roman Antiquities on the banks of the River Ribble within the site of the fort occupied by the Romans between 78 and 385 AD. Displays feature coins, pottery, Roman life and the famous Ribchester helmet. A large mural by Walter Kershaw (1983) depicts an accurate representation of life in the Roman fort of Bremetennacum and the adjoining settlement. There is also a selection of Roman inscriptions, carved stones and a display of Celtic heads. Behind the Museum are the excavated remains of the granaries.

Opening Times: March to October 2pm-5pm daily except June, July, August 11.30am-5.30pm daily November-February - Sundays only 2pm-4pm.

Booking Requirements: Party visits should be arranged in advance. Evening guided tours by arrangement.

Admission Charges: A charge is made for admission.

How to get there

Address: Ribchester Museum of Roman Antiquities, Riverside, Ribchester, Preston PR3 3XS.

Contact: Tel:Ribchester (025484) 261.

Location: On north side of River Ribble, NE of Preston. Take A59 Skipton/Clitheroe road and turn onto the B6245 for Ribchester.

Ordnance Survey Grid Reference: SD 650 350.

Parking: Village car park.

Public Transport: Served by bus links to Blackburn, Chipping, Preston, Longridge, Clitheroe and Whalley.

Facilities

Catering: None but available in village.

Toilets: Available at village car park.

Shelter: The Museum and its exhibits are under cover.

Disabled: There is minimal provision for the disabled at present, and no provision for the blind.

Average Length of Time Taken: Under an hour unless specialised study.

Group Size: About 30.

Leaflets/Books/Guides Available: Yes.

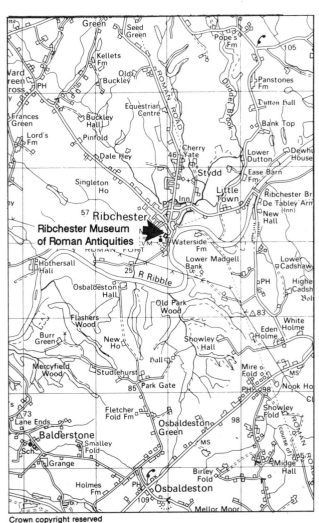

Crown copyright reserved

Rossendale Museum

Situated in pleasant parkland the Museum is housed in a Victorian mansion built in 1840 by the local mill-owning Hardman family. It was opened as a Museum in 1902. Exhibits on a variety of subjects especially Rossendale history, natural history, fine arts, ceramics, furniture, costume and foot wear. Regular temporary exhibitions programme, including the Rossendale Artists held in September. Lecture Room for 40 people; guided tours and lectures possible by arrangement.

Opening Times: Monday to Friday 1pm-5pm. Saturday 10am-noon, 1pm-5pm. Sunday, April to October 1pm-5pm. Bank Holidays - 1pm-5pm. Closed Christmas Day, Boxing Day, New Year's Day.

Booking Requirements: Party visits should be booked in advance.

Admission Charges: Free.

How to get there

Address: The Rossendale Museum, Whitaker Park, Haslingden Road, Rawtenstall, Rossendale BB4 6RE.

Contact: The Curator.
Tel: Rossendale (0706) 217777 or 226509.

Location: Situated in Whitaker Park, about a quarter of a mile from the large roundabout in Rawtenstall centre. The turning off to the Museum is on the right hand side of Haslingden Road, (A681) going towards Haslingden from Rawtenstall.

Ordnance Survey Grid Reference: SD 804 229.

Parking: A small car par for the use of visitors is on the right just inside the Museum's main gates. There is other parking nearby.

Public Transport: Accrington-Bacup bus stops in Haslingden Road near the park entrance.

Facilities

Catering: There is a small picnic area in the park.

Toilets: Available on the site.

Disabled Facilities: No special facilities for the disabled.

Average Length of Time Taken: Approximately one hour.

Leaflets/Books/Guides Available: A selection of books by local authors.

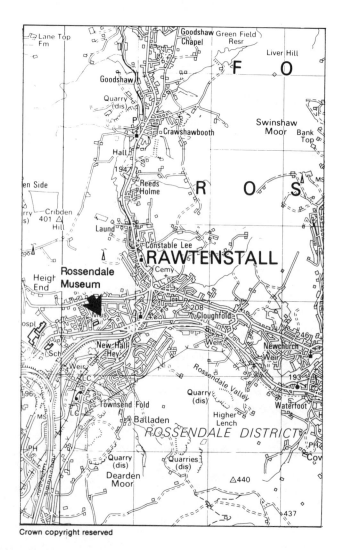

Crown copyright reserved

South Ribble Museum and Exhibition Centre

The Leyland free Grammar School was one of the earliest established in the County and dates from 1524. Much of the present building dates from c.1580 and is a fine example of the local timber framed construction technique. Though the school closed in 1876 the building continues to preserve a vivid picture of life in times past. Restored by the Local Authority in 1977 the Old Grammar School now houses on Exhibition Centre/Art Gallery and the Borough's Museum Collection.

Opening Times: Tuesday 10am-4pm. Thursday 1-4pm. Friday 10am-4pm. Saturday 10am-1pm. Closed Bank Holidays.

Booking Requirements: Groups (12 +) should notify custodian in advance.

Admission Charges: Free.

How to get there 40

Address: South Ribble Museum and Exhibition Centre, The Old Grammar School, Church Road, Leyland, Lancashire.

Contact: The Custodian.

Telephone: Preston (0772) 422041.

Location: Centre of Leyland, adjacent to St.Andrew's Parish Church on B5248.

Ordnance Survey Grid Reference: SD 540 216.

Parking: Main town centre car park opposite.

Public Transport: Nearest bus stop 'Leyland Cross' services to all areas.

Facilities

Catering: Town centre facilities close by.

Toilets: yes.

Disabled: No special provision.

Amount of time taken: 1hour.

Group Size: Parties of up to 30.

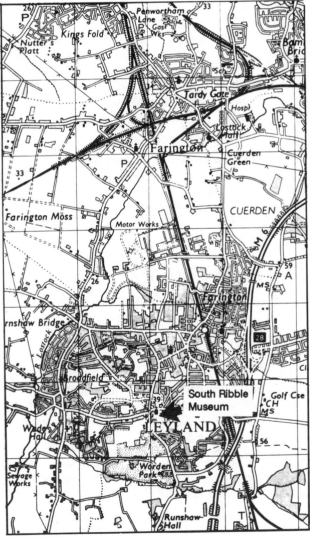

Crown copyright reserved

Steamtown Railway Centre

Over 30 preserved steam locomotives in the largest operating steam depot in the country, including the Lord Nelson, two Continental locomotives, and various others which visit. Interesting collection of restored coaches. On-site rides in coaches pulled by industrial locomotives along the 1 mile length of internal line (cost included in admission price). Miniature railway with 3 restored steam engines which were originally built at the beginning of the century pulling open carriages. A working model layout of railways, buses, trams and trolley buses is housed in a road coach as "A Model Transport Extravaganza". British Railways Collectors' Corner selling lamps, signs, badges, signals, etc. A well equipped repair workshop, an ash disposal tower, cranes and the last remaining working coaling plant in the British Isles are all on view outdoors with a signal box dating from 1876. The gift shop sells a vast range of items related to locomotives.

Opening Times: Daily from 9am to 5pm, except Christmas period. Winter (October - Easter) 10am to 4pm.

Admission Charges: These depend on the availability of steam engine rides. "In Steam" admission prices are higher but include all costs of rides on steam hauled standard and 15 inch railway. Locomotives are in steam on Sundays from Easter to October and daily in July and August.

How to get there 41

Address: Warton Road, Carnforth, Lancashire LA5 9HX.

Contact: Visits Manager.
Telephone: Carnforth (0524) 734220.

Location: Approximately 1/2 mile from the centre of Carnforth on the Warton Road. Carnforth is 7 miles north of Lancaster on the A6. When approaching from the M6 leave at exit 35, a half mile north of Carnforth.

Ordnance Survey Grid Reference: SD 495 712.

Parking: A large car park is available adjacent to the site with free parking for patrons. Coach parking is available near the site.

Public Transport: Steamtown is situated some 200 yards from Carnforth railway station to which there are regular services from Lancaster, Barrow and the north. There are regular bus services to Carnforth from Lancaster, Morecambe and Kendal.

Facilities

Food and Drink: Refreshments in a Gresley buffet car at the platform. A grassed picnic site is available at the south end of the site.

Toilets: These are situated near to Collectors' Corner.

Shelter: Many of the locomotives are housed in a large engine shed where they can be viewed by the public in wet or cold weather.

Disabled: The disabled and handicapped are welcome at Steamtown and a great deal of enjoyment can be derived particularly when the locomotives are in steam. It must be pointed out that the ground surface is rough and makes the manoeuvring of wheelchairs difficult. Wheelchairs can be accommmodated in the ladies toilet on the site.

Average Length of Stay: Up to a whole day.

Miscellaneous: Steam excursions from Carnforth are run in conjunction with British Rail. Substantial reductions can be achieved, however, if a large party charters a train. Each train has 400 seats. Further details available from the above address or British Rail. Guided tours of Steamtown are available and when booked in advance the tours can be planned to suit the specialist requirements of smaller groups.

Leaflets/Books/Guides Available: Steamtown Guide and a wide selection of books concerning steam engines and trains are on sale in the gift shop.

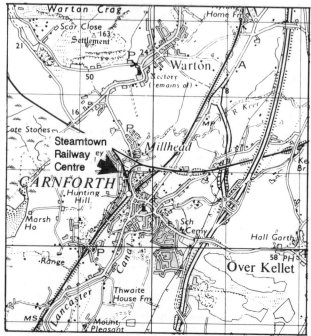

Crown copyright reserved

The Weavers' Triangle Visitor Centre

The Weavers' Triangle provides a fascinating town trail of the industrial heritage in Burnley. The area straddles the Leeds and Liverpool Canal, which reached Burnley around 1800. Industry developed along the banks after 1840, when mills were allowed to take water for use in their steam engine boilers. The Canal is carried above the Burnley valley on a huge embankment known as "The Burnley Mile" giving wide views of Pendle Hill and the Pennines. By the end of the 19th century, Burnley was one of the world's foremost cotton weaving centres. The area contains a remarkably well preserved Victorian industrial townscape and the Trail indicates some of the many interesting features such as the multi-storey spinning mills, single storey weaving sheds, an iron works which once housed one of the area's largest steam engine makers and millwrights, weavers' cottages and an imposing Canal wharf and warehouses. Several of these are statutory listed buildings. Some of the most significant buildings by the Canal have plaques giving their name, date of building and original use. A guided tour service is operated by members of the Friends of the Weavers' Triangle, and Canal boat trips can be arranged. The Visitor Centre is the former Wharfmaster's house and Canal Toll House.

Admission Charges: Free, donations welcomed. Charges for guided tours.

Open: The Canal towpath is open at all times. The Visitor Centre is open Saturday, Sunday, Tuesday, Wednesday, and most Bank Holidays 2pm to 4pm and at other times by arrangement.

Booking Requirements: Group visits and those requiring guided tours.

How to get there 42

Address: 85, Manchester Road, Burnley BB11 1JZ.

Contact: The Friends of the Weavers' Triangle. Tel.Burnley (0282)30055 - Tourist Information Centre.

Location: The Visitor Centre is only 5minutes walk from the town centre. There are many access points to the Canal.

Ordnance Survey Grid Reference: SD 838 323.

Parking: Ample public parking facilities are available nearby.

Public Transport: The bus and railway stations are a short walk away.

Facilities

Catering: Light refreshments at the Visitor Centre, town centre facilities.

Toilets: Yes, and at Burnley bus station and Burnley Mechanics TIC.

Disabled: Access to the Visitor Centre is by a narrow flight of stone steps. The Canal towpath has a reasonable surface.

Average Length of Stay: Visitor Centre and Weavers' Triangle about 1 1/2 hours.

Group size: No limit, though 30maximum to view the Visitor Centre.

Leaflets/Books/Guides: Along t'Cut - R. Frost. Weavers' Triangle - A visitors guide - R.Frost and B. Hall.

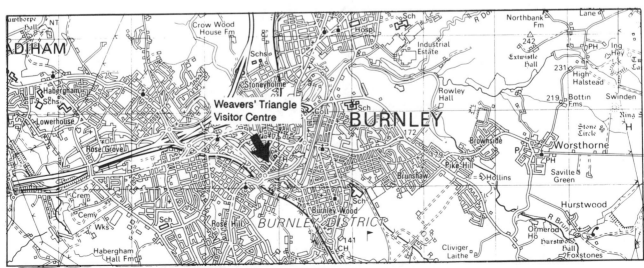

Crown copyright reserved

Lancashire's Early Industrial Heritage

Published by the Lancashire County Planning Department in March 1983 on sale throughout the County, *price £1.25.*

This booklet attempts to explain the significance of the buildings and machinery which are the most easily inspected parts of Lancashire's early industrial heritage by telling the story of the Industrial evolution between the approximate dates 1750 and 1850 and within the present County boundaries.

Ordnance Survey Grid References are given for all the more important and easily visible sites referred to in the booklet.

Country Parks

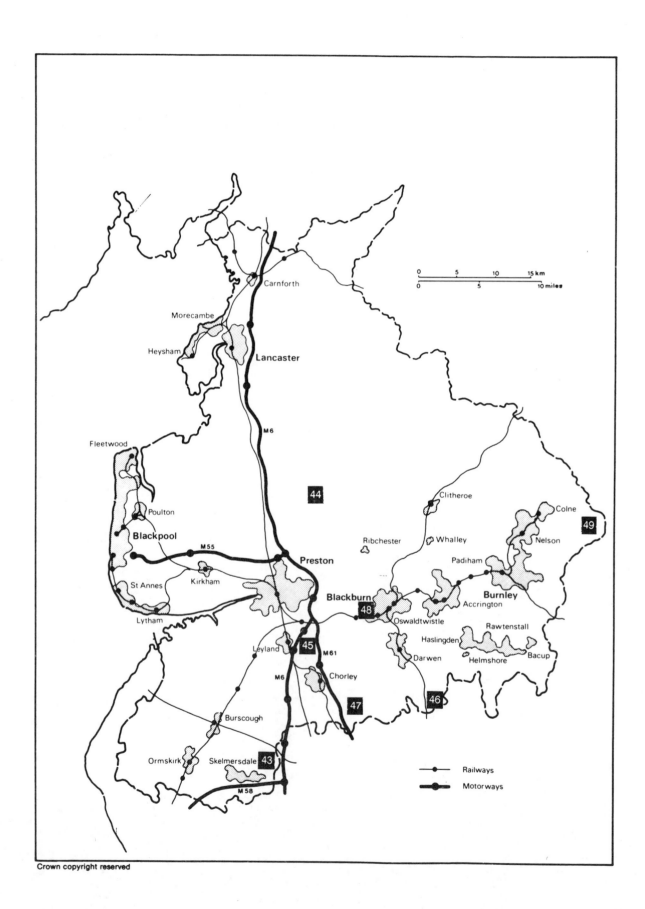

Carnforth

Morecambe

Heysham

Lancaster

M 6

Fleetwood

44

Clitheroe

Colne

49

Poulton

Ribchester

Whalley

Nelson

Blackpool

M 55

Padiham

St Annes

Kirkham

Blackburn

48

Burnley

Accrington

Lytham

Oswaldtwistle

Rawtenstall

Leyland

45

M 61

Haslingden

Darwen

Helmshore

Bacup

M 6

Chorley

47

46

Burscough

Ormskirk

Skelmersdale

43

Railways

M 58

Motorways

0   5   10   15 km
0   5   10 miles

Beacon Country Park

Beacon Country Park comprises 304 acres of open countryside within walking distance of Skelmersdale. It lies on the upper slopes of a ridge facing south west and at Ashurst Beacon in particular there are magnificent views over the West Lancashire Plain, the Irish Sea, and inland to the Pennine Moors. The landscape is mainly wild flower meadows and rolling pastures separated by former boundary hedges, some of which may well date back hundreds of years. Plantations of pine trees and semi-mature oak woods provide a home for a variety of wildlife, particularly birds and insects. There is a nature trail following distinct paths through the Park. Beacon Park Visitor Centre incorporates an exhibition area open to the public and to educational study groups, and features displays illustrating a variety of countryside areas.

Opening Times: Seven days a week all the year round.
Booking Requirements: For events and activities contact the Ranger Service. Bookings for meetings at the Visitor Centre, Craft Fairs, Caravan clubs and outdoor events from the Ranger Service.

Admission Charges: None. Charges made for some special events and for courses, talks and walks.

How to get there 43

Address: Beacon Park Visitor Centre, Beacon Lane, Dalton, Wigan WN8 7RU.

Contact: The Countryside Ranger Service.
Tel:Up Holland (0695) 622794.

Location: Beacon Country Park is located to the east of Skelmersdale and is close to the M6-M58 Junction. The Visitor Centre is situated on Elmers Green Lane just off Beacon Lane between Dalton and UpHolland. Access also via numerous footpaths leading into the Park from the south and west.

Ordnance Survey Grid Reference: SD 502 070.

Parking: There are four main car parks off Beacon Lane on the east side of the Park including one at the Visitor Centre.

Public Transport: The Park is not well served by public transport. There is a limited bus service from Orrell via Tontine, contact Ranger Service for details.

Facilities

Catering: Fully licensed public bar serving full and snack meals. Refreshment bar with soft drinks, tea, coffee, and cold snacks. Picnic tables have been provided throughout the Park.

Toilets: Good facilities in the Visitor Centre.

Shelter: Visitor Centre.

Disabled: The Centre has a disabled toilet and ramps for wheelchairs throughout. Some of the trails are accessible by wheelchair in dry weather but there are some fairly steep hills.

Amount of time taken: Up to a full day.

Group size: Up to 30 for guided walks.

Leaflets/Books/Guides: Maps of Beacon Country Park. Orienteering maps.

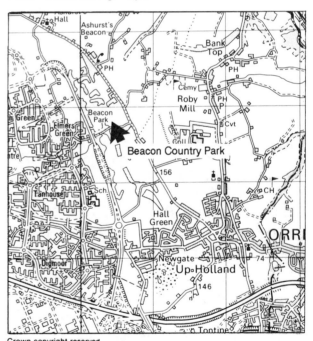

Crown copyright reserved

Beacon Fell Country Park

A 185 acre Country Park with an extensive network of footpaths in open countryside or through conifer plantations. There are six car parks, picnic areas, and the Carwags Information Centre where refreshments are available during the summer months. The views from Beacon Fell over the Bowland Fells and across the Lancashire Plain to the coast are amongst the most attractive in the country. The winter scenery can be particularly attractive and many people, especially walkers, visit the Country Park throughout the year.

Booking Requirements: It is important for parties wanting a guided walk/talk by the Ranger to make arrangements well in advance; at least one month's notice is advisable.

Admission Charges: None.

Opening Times: No restrictions.

How to get there 44

Address: Beacon Fell Country Park, Nr.Goosnargh, Preston.

Contact: The Countryside Officer, Property Services Department, East Cliff County Offices, Preston PR1 3ET. Tel:Preston (0772) 263896.

Location: Located 8 miles north of Preston. Signposted from Longridge, Broughton (on A6, 3 miles north of Preston) and Brock Bridge on A6, 14 miles south of Lancaster.

Ordnance Survey Grid Reference: SD 568 428.

Parking: Six free car parks are situated throughout the Country Park. All are fairly small and not able to accommodate large coaches. However, it is possible for coaches to use the roads leading up to the Fell and to drop people off at the layby in front of Fell House picnic site. Fell roads are not suitable for coaches.

Public Transport: There is no public transport to the Park, but from Preston there are bus services to Chipping and Brock (on A6) from which the walking distances are 4 miles and 5 miles respectively.

Facilities

Toilets: Toilets are situated at Fell House and Carwags Information Centre, possible for wheelchairs to be accommodated.

Shelter: There is no shelter on the Fell apart from Carwags Information Centre which is only open occasionally. There are no facilities for eating packed lunches inside.

Special Equipment Needed: It is advisable to take waterproof footwear and rainwear if walking any distance. Special care should be taken during the winter.

Disabled: It is not normally practicable for wheelchairs to be taken beyond the perimeter road and car parks. However, access to the Quarry picnic site and tables is possible with assistance and in dry weather Larch Avenue, although fairly steep, could be used with help. All other paths are fairly steep, sometimes with steps, and are often wet or muddy. Some of the smaller car parks are secluded from the roads, are quiet and have good viewpoints. Toilets with provision for the disabled are located at Fell House picnic site and Carwags Information Centre.

Average Length of Time Taken: Approximately a half day trip with guide but visits for fieldwork could be expected to last longer.

Group Size: No real limit in terms of space.

Leaflets/Books/Guides: Yes.

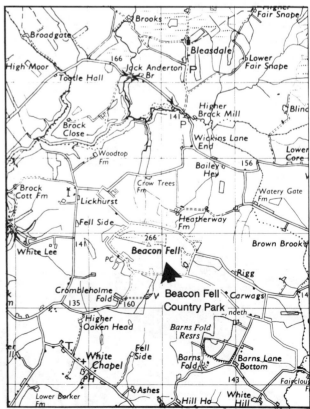

Crown copyright reserved

Cuerden Valley Park

A Country Park of largely unspoilt character with much of the land still actively farmed. There is a wealth of trees, wildflowers, birds and other wildlife, and an extensive network of surfaced footpaths. The agricultural land in the Park is mainly used for grazing sheep and cattle. Cereals are grown in a small area at the south end. The River Lostock meanders through the length of the Park with open access to it at many points. Most of the grass near the river is left to grow long then cut for hay in summer. In the centre of the Park is an attractive lake built in the 19th century to provide water for Cuerden Hall. It has been stocked with coarse fish. Mallard, moorhen and heron are often seen as well as dragonflies and frogs. There are several established woods of varying character and further areas have been planted with mainly native species of trees and shrubs. Bluebells and rhododendrons colour the woods in early summer and ferns are abundant in July and August. The diversity of habitats within the Park provides for many birds including woodpeckers, long tailed tits and several kinds of warblers.

Booking Requirements: Groups and school parties are advised to contact the Ranger Service in advance.

Admission Charges: None. Fishing is only allowed by permit (see Miscellaneous section).

Opening Times: Access is available at all times.

How to get there 45

Address: Cuerden Valley Park Wildlife Centre, Shady Lane, Bamber Bridge, Preston PR5 6AU.

Contact: The Ranger Service.

Tel.Preston (0772) 324129.

Location: South of Preston near Bamber Bridge and Whittle-le-Woods. Easy access from M6 and M61.

Parking: Coaches are advised to use the larger Town Brow entrance on B5256, but contact the Ranger Service. Several car parks.

Ordnance Survey Grid Reference: SD 567 237.

Public Transport: British Rail station about 1 mile away in Bamber Bridge. Bus services from Preston, Chor-

ley and Leyland to Clayton-le-Woods, Bamber Bridge and Whittle-le-Woods.

Facilities

Catering: Picnic tables and many other spots for picnicking. Coffee Shop at Cuerden Hall (Sue Ryder Foundation).

Toilets: None in the Park but public toilets can be found in Bamber Bridge town centre.

Shelter: None.

Disabled: Most footpaths will accommodate wheelchairs but steep sections are stepped. Disabled toilets at the Park Centre. Special arrangements are available for disabled fishermen - details from Ranger Service.

Miscellaneous Information: Fishing is not allowed without a permit which can be obtained in advance from: R.E. and J.M.Robertson, Newsagents, 2 Spinners Square, Station Road, Bamber Bridge.

Leaflets/Books/Guides: Cuerden Valley Park - leaflet .

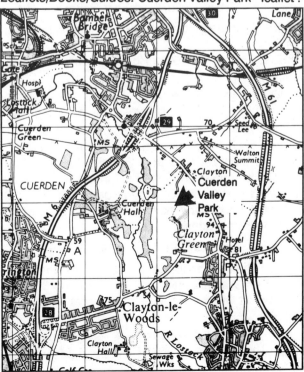

Crown copyright reserved

53

Jumbles Country Park

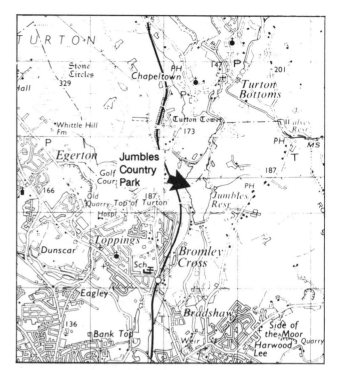

Crown copyright reserved

Just 4 miles from Bolton on the Burnley road, this small country park lies in the thinly-wooded Bradshaw Valley. There is much for the visitors to see and do, including a choice of two trails, and many birds and plants to be found at different seasons mean interesting walks are assured. There are fine views around the reservoir (55 acres) and a network of footpaths radiate up the valley and across adjacent hills. A comprehensive programme of guided walks and activities is organised by the WPM Information Service.

Opening Times: Information Centre opens Winter, Sunday only, 10am-dusk or 5pm. Easter to October, Wednesday and Saturday 1pm-5pm, Sunday 11am-6pm, Bank Holidays 10am-6pm.

Booking Requirements: Fishing permits from Ranger or NWWA. Any formal event or activity in the area requires permission from the NWWA. Enquire through the WPM Information Service.

Admission Charges: No charge.

How to get there 46

Address: Jumbles Information Centre, Waterfold Car Park, off Bradshaw Road, Bradshaw, Bolton.

Contact: The Ranger or West Pennine Moors Information Service.
Tel:Bolton (0204) 853360 or Horwich (0204) 691549.

Location: The Jumbles Reservoir is situated in the Bradshaw Valley on the north western periphery of Greater Manchester. The Country Park can be reached from either of the main roads which run parallel with the valley on either side of the Reservoir. The B6391 to the west runs from Bromley Cross northwards past Jumbles, Wayoh, and Turton and Entwistle Reservoirs to the A666 Blackburn road. The A676 on the east side forms the main cross country route from Bolton to Ramsbottom and Burnley.

Ordnance Survey Grid Reference: SD 735 145.

Parking: There are at present two car parks in the Jumbles area at Waterfold (80 cars) (location - OS SD 731 143), and at Ousel Nest (50+ cars) (location OS SD 737 140).

Public Transport: Bromley Cross railway station is within walking distance of the Park and is on the main line between Blackburn, Bolton and Manchester. Bus services to Bromley Cross from Bolton, Darwen and Blackburn. The Bolton-Burnley service stops at the south east corner access road.

Facilities

Catering: No formal catering facilities, but picnicking is allowed in the Park and picnic tables are provided at Waterfold car park and at scattered points around the Park.

Toilets: At present toilet facilities exist only at Waterfold car park.

Shelter: None in the Park.

Special Equipment Needed: Boots and waterproofs necessary in wet weather.

Disabled: There are special invalid car parking spaces at Waterfold car park, plus a disabled toilet. Special bird hide with wheelchair access.

Leaflets/Books/Guides: A considerable number are available.

Rivington

A proposed Country Park adjacent to Lower Rivington Reservoirs with extensive areas of rural parkland and meadow, and including the former Rivington Hall Estate. The historic village of Rivington has a Church built about 1540 and remodelled about 1666, and a Unitarian Chapel built in 1703. There are trails and numerous walks and from the vantage point of Rivington Pike (1,191feet above sea level), the site of a former beacon, there are magnificent views over the moors and the Lancashire Plain. A "ruined castle" on the shore of the Lower Rivington Reservoir is a replica of the ruins of Liverpool Castle. The extensive Ornamental Japanese and Italian Gardens were laid out by Lord Leverhulme on the western downslope of the Pike, and are now being restored after many years of neglect. The west front of Rivington Hall was rebuilt in 1774 and on the west side of the court there is a date stone of 1694. The Hall Barn and the Great House Barn - at each end of the long straight Drive to the Hall - are both unique in the north of England. Although the exteriors are much restored, the interiors are the original 17th century cruck structures. Both Barns now house refreshment facilities with the Hall Barn also having a function room whilst the Great House Barn houses a new Visitor information Centre. The proposed Rivington Country Park is in the area which was designated as Lever Park at the beginning of the century and was bequeathed by Act of Parliament by Lord Leverhulme to the public for their recreation. The land has, therefore, functioned as a Country Park throughout this century.

Opening Times: Great House Barn Information Centre, Easter to October, daily 10am-5pm; November to March, Saturday, Sunday 10am-5pm or dusk, Wednesday 1pm-5pm or dusk.

Booking Requirements: Any formal activity or event in the area requires permission from NWWA, enquire at the Information Centre.

How to get there 47

Address: Great House Barn Information Centre, Rivington Lane, Horwich BL6 7SB.

Contact: West Pennine Moors Information Service, Tel:Horwich (0204) 691549.

Location: Between Chorley, Horwich and Adlington and adjacent to the Rivington reservoirs. The Park can be approached from Horwich by way of Lever Park Avenue (offA673), from Anderton and Adlington by way of Babylon Lane and Horrobin Lane to Rivington Church, from Belmont by way of Sheephouse Lane.

Ordnance Survey Grid Reference: SD 630 140.

Parking: Free car parks are located throughout the Park.

Public Transport: There is a regular service from Bolton to Lever Park gates and a weekday service between Chorley and Horwich. The Adlington and Blackrod railway stations on the Manchester-Preston line are both about 1 1/2miles from the Park.

Facilities

Catering: Refreshments daily at Great House Barn and Sundays only at the Hall Barn.

Toilets: At Great House Barn, at the Hall Barn (Sundays), and at the Terraced Gardens (Easter to October, dawn - dusk).

Shelter: At Great House Barn Information Centre.

Special Equipment Needed: Stout footwear is advisable for longer walks.

Disabled: Toilets at Great House Barn. The Information Centre in Great House Barn has been designed with the disabled in mind.

Leaflets/Books/Guides: A substantial number of books, leaflets, self guided trails is available at West Pennine Moors Information Centres. Annual programme of guided walks.

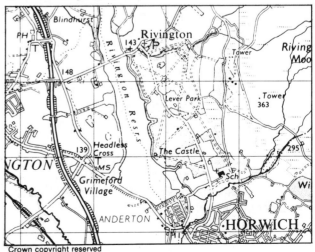

Crown copyright reserved

Witton Country Park

Country and woodland walks, tree trail and nature trail (with illustrated guides), picnic sites, ponds, panoramic views from the highest points; fun and fitness course, horse trail, children's play area, general recreation areas. Visitor Centre with local and natural history exhibitions; stables, farm tools and horse drawn carriage exhibitions; cafeteria; craft shop; lecture theatre; educational tours (by prior arrangement).

Opening Times: Country Park open daily throughout the year. The Visitor Centre is open all year, Thursday, Friday and Saturday (1pm-5pm) Sunday, Bank Holidays, local holidays (11am-5pm).

Booking Requirements: For educational visits and tours advance booking with the Warden is necessary, particularly in summer when tours are popular.

Admission: Free to Visitor Centre and Country Park.

How to get there 48

Address: Witton Country Park, Preston Old Road, Blackburn BB2 2TP.

Contact: Mr.R.Wilson (Senior Warden). Tel:Blackburn (0254) 55423.

Location: Approximately 2 miles west of Blackburn and 8 miles east of M6 Junction 31. Easily accessible from both main roads linking Blackburn and Preston. The Visitor Centre is located on the southern edge of the Park, and is best approached via the A674, Preston Old Road.

Ordnance Survey Grid Reference: SD 662 274.

Parking: Car parking facilities free at several sites around the Park. Free coach parking at the main entrance at Preston Old Road.

Public Transport: Regular service from Blackburn centre on two bus routes also services from Preston and Chorley. Blackburn railway station 2 miles; Mill Hill and Cherry Tree stations 1 mile.

Facilities

Catering: Cafeteria at weekends and Bank Holidays.

Toilets: Available at the Visitor Centre, and at the Preston Old Road entrance.

Shelter: Indoor accommodation when Visitor Centre open.

Disabled: Only a few of the paths are suitable for wheelchairs. Disabled toilet facilities at the main entrance off Preston Old Road. Most of the Visitor Centre is easily accessible.

Group Sizes: Any size group, suitably supervised, can be accommodated in the Park, but the lecture theatre accommodates a maximum of 50 people.

Leaflets/Books/Guides: Various, including Birds of Witton Country Park, Nature Trail,Tree Trail, The Feildens of Witton Park

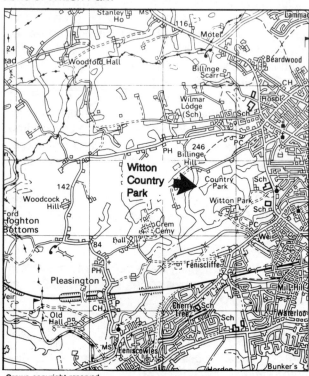

Crown copyright reserved

Wycoller Country Park

Clapper Bridge and Pack-Horse Bridge

A Country Park and conservation area enclosing the Wycoller Estate and hamlet where a settlement can be traced back to between 1,000 and 3,000BC. The area has great scenic and historic interest and, through its association with the Brontes, also has considerable literary interest. The settlement developed in the 17th century as a weaving community but declined in the 18th and 19th centuries following the invention of the power-loom which led to the relocation of industry in other places. Wycoller Hall, built by the Hartley family about the end of the 16th century, was deserted in 1818 and the rest of the hamlet was later abandoned. The ruins of the Hall are reputed to be the Ferndean Manor of Charlotte Bronte's novel Jane Eyre. The local water board acquired the area in 1890 with the intention of flooding the valley as a reservoir. This was never carried out and for the next 80 years or so Wycoller was in effect fossilised. The County Council bought the Estate in 1973 and since then has encouraged a gradual and carefully managed restoration which is recreating the hamlet as a living community. The pasture and moorland slopes were once clothed with oak forest but today the woodland is concentrated in the stream valleys. A network of paths give magnificent views from the tops above Bank House and Copy House, or the peace and tranquility of the Dene. The Clapper Bridge and Pack-Horse Bridge are two ancient and unique features, and the Aisled Barn, formerly the coach house for the Hall, has been carefully restored for use as an Information Centre.

Opening Times: No restrictions.

Booking Requirements: None.

Admission Charges: None.

How to get there 49

Address: Wycoller Country Park, Wycoller, Nr.Colne.
Location: Three miles east of Colne. From the town centre follow A6068 (for Keighley) for 3/4 mile, turn right for Trawden on B6250, 1/4 mile further on turn left through Winewall and follow the signs to Wycoller. From Haworth the road across the Keighley Moors joins the A6068 at Laneshawbridge to the east of the above A6068/B6250 junction.
Ordnance Survey Grid Reference: SD 926 395.
Parking: The car park is 1/3 mile from the village and Country Park. To prevent traffic congestion in the village, cars (unless driven by a registered disabled

person) are not permitted beyond the car park.
Public Transport: Regular bus services from Burnley/Colne to Laneshawbridge or Trawden, thence by public footpath (1 to 1 1/2 miles) to Wycoller

Facilities

Toilets: Yes.

Special Equipment Needed: It is recommended that stout footwear is worn and waterproof clothing is taken.

Disabled: Cars driven by registered disabled are permitted to drive beyond the car park to have access to Wycoller where there are limited parking spaces near the picnic tables and toilet block adjacent to the ruined Hall. The toilet block has a disabled toilet.

Shelter: There is very little shelter in the Country Park other than in the Information Centre.

Miscellaneous Information: Wycoller Country Park can be divided into two areas - the environs of the hamlet, and the adjoining farmland where sheep and cattle are grazed all the year round and hay is harvested in the summer. Public access throughout most of the Park is, therefore, restricted to the footpaths; there are also several longer-distance footpaths passing outside the Park. Three circular walks have been waymarked. It must, however, be remembered that outside the Country Park the land is privately owned and walking is restricted to the statutory footpaths. Extra care is particularly necessary during the lambing season (approximately March and April).

Leaflets/Books/Guides: Yes.

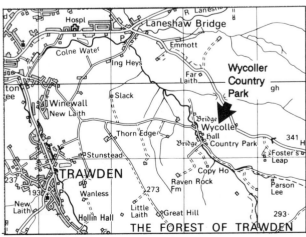

Crown copyright reserved

Nature Reserves
and Zoos

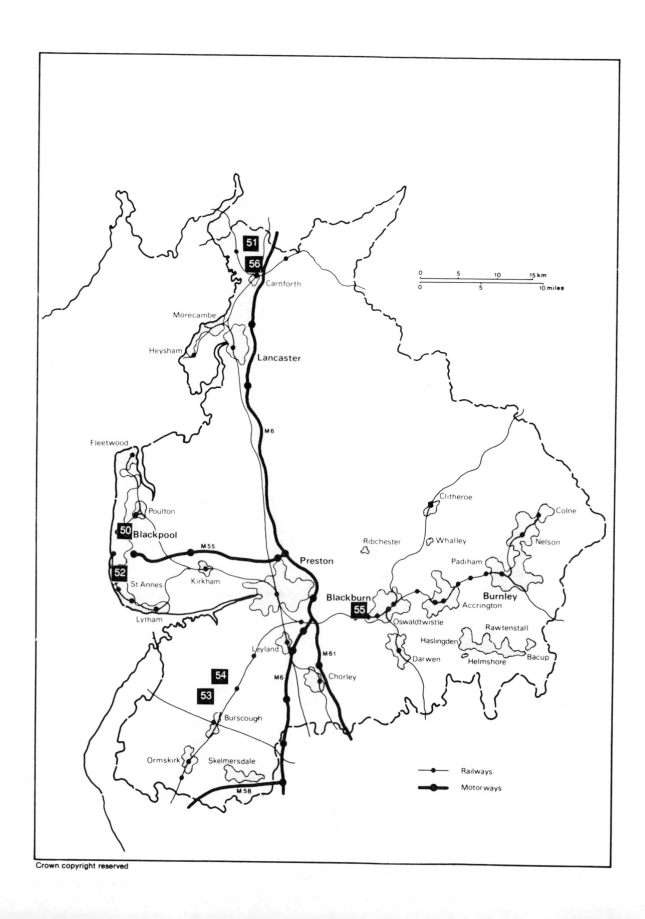

Blackpool Zoo

The Zoo covers 32 acres and has a collection which contains many of the popular animals together with those which are not so well known. The invigorating open aspect of this zoo without bars has been widely acclaimed, whilst the high standard of care is reflected in the vitality of the animals. The sea lions swim and perform in the finest pool in Europe. A comprehensive labelling system and information panels give details of specific groups of animals. A miniature railway operates through attractively landscaped areas close to some of the animal enclosures.

Catering and Picnicking Facilities - full catering services from Easter to the beginning of November - Licensed Restaurant, Cafeteria and Snack Bars - Restaurant telephone - Blackpool 65936. Menus and booking forms available from: The Manager, J.L.Catering, Zoo Restaurant. During the winter months hot drinks and snacks are on sale.

Opening Times: Open every day except Christmas Day. Winter months 10am-4.30pm, summer months 10am-6pm. Feeding times: sea lions 11am and 3.30pm, penguins 11.30am and 3.pm.

Booking Requirements: Reduced prices of admission are available to groups of 25 and over if booked in advance. Booking forms on request.

Admission Charges: A charge is made for admission. Reductions for parties.

How to get there 50

Address: Blackpool Municipal Zoological Gardens, East Park Drive, Blackpool FY3 8PP.

Contact: The Education Officer, The Zoo School, Municipal Zoological Gardens, East Park Drive, Blackpool FY3 8PP. Tel:Blackpool (0253) 65027 Ext.46.

Location: Situated off East Park Drive, main entrance and car park on Woodside Drive. Approximately two miles from M55 motorway. The Zoo is well signposted from all main roads leading into the resort.

Ordnance Survey Grid Reference: SD 335 360.

Parking: Parking for 3,000 cars. Free parking for buses and coaches.

Public Transport: Within Blackpool, the No.21 bus service provides an in-season direct link between the sea front (from Adelaide Street close to the Tower) and the Zoo main entrance. The 15a service runs via Victoria Hospital to the Zoo main entrance during the season.

Facilities

Toilets: Several toilet blocks including for disabled persons.

Shelter: In case of bad weather, many animals may be studied in covered accommodation in the Ape House, the Large Mammal House, the Monkey House and the Tree Kangaroo House.

Disabled: Full facilities including the free use of wheelchairs.

Average Length of Time Taken: Several hours.

Group Sizes: No limits although the School Classroom has only 80 seats.

Leaflets/Books/Guides: Zoo Guide.

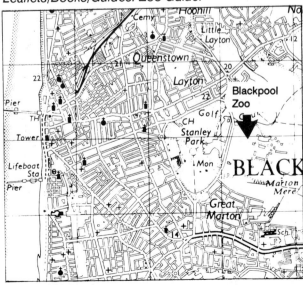

Crown copyright reserved

Leighton Moss RSPB Reserve

The Reserve occupies 321 acres of the floor of a small, unspoilt and attractively wooded valley flanked by limestone hills. A variety of habitats include reedbeds, open water and mature woodland; three main meres and four small ones. 207 species of birds have been recorded in the area and 74 have bred there. Red deer, foxes, badgers and red squirrels frequent the Reserve and weasels, stoats and other small mammals are seen regularly. There are seven bird watching hides and a nature trail. Visitor Centre has displays and exhibitions and slide presentation. Shop has a selection of books and gifts. Binoculars for hire

Opening Times: Every day except Tuesdays throughout the year, 9am to dusk. Visitor Centre open Sunday, Wednesday, Thursday, Saturday, Bank Holidays, 10am-5pm, and for school parties on other days.

Booking Requirements: Advance bookings for parties of ten and over must be made with the Warden.

Admission Charges: A charge is made for admission. Members of RSPB and Young Ornithologists Club free.

How to get there 51

Address: Leighton Moss Nature Reserve, Silverdale, Carnforth, Lancaster LA5 0SW.

Contact: Senior Warden, Tel:Silverdale (0524) 701601 or 701413.

Location: Close to the NE tip of Morecambe Bay between the villages of Silverdale and Yealand Redmayne. The Visitor Centre is situated on the road from Yealand Redmayne to Silverdale just before the railway station.

Ordnance Survey Grid Reference: SD 478 751.

Parking: For cars and coaches by the Visitor Centre.

Public Transport: Bus from Lancaster to Silverdale. Rail to Silverdale.

Facilities

Catering: None. There is a small picnic area next to the car park at the Visitor Centre. Shop sells snacks.

Toilets: In the Visitor Centre.

Special Equipment Needed: Sensible footwear and water-proofs for outdoor work.

Disabled: Two hides are specially equipped.

Amount of Time Taken: A morning or afternoon.

Group Size: Any within reason but parties usually split into groups of 10 to 12 and escorted by Reserve staff.

Leaflets/Books/Guides: Leighton Moss Reserve Guide. Wide selection of books available at the shop.

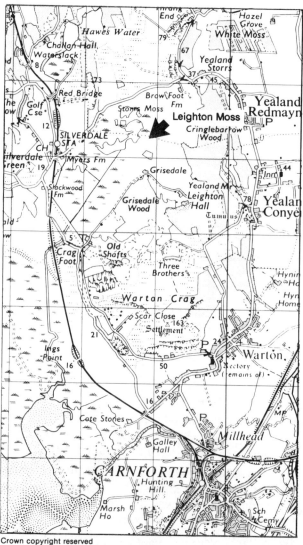

Crown copyright reserved

62

Lytham St. Annes Nature Reserve

Established in 1968, the Reserve is of prime importance as a scientific site; as a historic remnant of a previously much more extensive dune system; as an amenity area for public use and as a rich area for educational use. The Reserve is completely open - you may walk where you will but do not disturb or damage plants or wildlife. There is a wide variety of wild plants, insects, small mammals and birds.

Opening Times: Daylight hours.

Booking Requirements: Party bookings.

Admission Charges: None.

How to get there 52

Address: Clifton Drive North, St.Annes-on-Sea, Lytham St.Annes.

Contact: Parks Superintendent. Tel:St.Annes (0253) 721222.

Location: Bounded by Clifton North, Pontins Holiday Camp, Kilgrimol Gardens and the railway line, lying between the northern part of Lytham St.Annes and Blackpool South Shore.

Ordnance Survey Grid Reference: SD 308 307.

Parking: Roadside.

Public Transport: Local bus services between the Blackpool and Lytham.

Facilities

Catering: Not on site. Nearest probably at South Shore.

Toilets: None.

Shelter: None.

Disabled: No special facilities.

Amount of Time Taken: Casual visitor 30 minutes, specialist interest can be longer.

Group Size: 10-20. Parties can be accommodated on Wednesday and Sunday afternoons.

Leaflets/Books/Guides: Illustrated guide book from the Parks Office (292 Clifton Drive South).

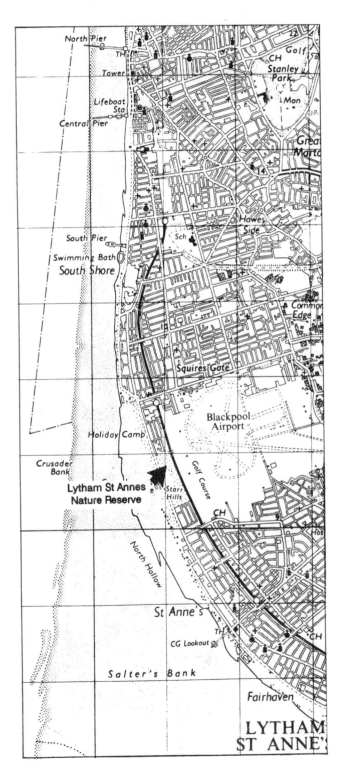

Martin Mere
Wildfowl Trust

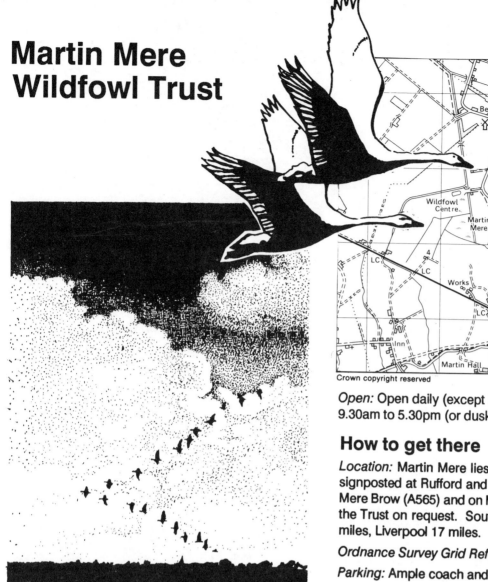

Crown copyright reserved

Open: Open daily (except 24 and 25December), 9.30am to 5.30pm (or dusk if earlier).

How to get there 53

Location: Martin Mere lies in West Lancashire and is signposted at Rufford and at Burscough (A59) and at Mere Brow (A565) and on M6. A map is available from the Trust on request. Southport 10 miles, Preston 14 miles, Liverpool 17 miles.

Ordnance Survey Grid Reference: SD 428 144.

Parking: Ample coach and car parking.

Public Transport: Burscough railway station on the Southport-Wigan-Manchester line, less than 2 miles from Martin Mere. Bus service operates 2 hourly from Ormskirk via Burscough. Details from Liverpool (051) 933 8333.

Contact: Sharon Ament, PRO, Tel: Burscough (0704) 895181.

Address: Martin Mere Wildfowl Trust, Burscough, Ormskirk L40 0TA.

Facilities

Food and Drink: Coffee bar/snack facilities. Picnic areas with tables and benches.

Toilets: Adequate facilities, including access for the disabled.

Shelter: Most of the attractions are outside but there is shelter within the Visitor Centre

Disabled: Full facilities are available for the disabled including the free use of wheelchairs. For the visually handicapped there is a trail with braille notices and aromatic shrubs and also a cassette facility available free of charge.

Average Length of Stay: Half to full day.

Leaflets/Books/Guides: Yes,including Martin Mere Souvenir Guidebook. Educational Discovery Sheets. Termly Magazines. Species and Information Lists.

Group Size: No limits.

Martin Mere covers 363 acres of marsh and meadow. The waterfowl gardens extend over 45 acres of landscaped pens and pools containing over 1,600 tame and free flying wildfowl of 120 species from many parts of the world, together with flocks of Chilean Flamingos and Greater Flamingos. The Mere is a large man-made lake covering some 20 acres. The water attracts many thousands of wild birds which can be viewed at close quarters from spacious observation hides. The Wild Refuge covers about 260 acres over which a number of hides provide spectacular viewing, particularly in winter when it is visited by many thousands of ducks and Pink-footed Geese, as well as numbers of Whooper and Bewick's Swans. There is a well stocked Gift Shop with one of the best selections of natural history books in the north west. The Visitor Centre is a Norwegian-style log construction with views over Flamingo Pool and Swan Lake; Lecture Theatre/Cinema and Brass Rubbing Centre. There is also a gallery which displays work of local artists in various media. A nominal charge is made for guided tours. Lectures are undertaken by members of the Wildfowl Trust Staff, many and varied events are presented, and a series of ten lectures is held annually on a conservation theme.

Admission Charges: A charge is made for admission. Party rates for groups of 20 and over. Guided tours and film shows must be booked in advance.

Mere Sands Wood Nature Reserve

This site is classified as an S.S.S.I for its geological interest, providing the best sections in the Shirdley Hill Sand of Lancashire. Peripheral woodland of birch and oak, a sizeable stand of Scots Pine, considerable areas of open water, and areas of scrub, dry and wet heath make up the site. There are good breeding populations of many types of birds attracted by the woodland and the lake and there are spring and autumn migrants. Large and small mammals include the red squirrel, fox and the open heath areas abound with flowering plants. A small education unit with classroom facilities enables practical field studies to be followed by more formal training.

Opening Times: Information Centre, car park and toilet open each day 10am-5pm. This Reserve is closed at certain times, particularly the breeding season.

Booking Requirements: Large parties by arrangement with warden.

Admission Charges: Free.

How to get there 54

Address: Holmeswood Road, Rufford, Ormskirk, Lancashire.

Contact: Warden:J.Parkinson.
Telephone:Rufford (0704) 821809.

Location: 1 mile west of Rufford on B5246 Holmeswood Road. Turn off A59 Liverpool-Preston Road at Hesketh Arms Rufford. Reserve access 1 mile on left via cart track clearly signed. Public footpath via Rufford cricket ground or via two public footpaths direct from B5246.

Ordnance Survey Grid Reference: SD 448 162.

Parking: On site, restricted to 35 vehicles.

Public Transport: By bus or rail via Ormskirk-Preston to Rufford, bus stops at the Hesketh Arms. Southport bus service infrequent along Holmeswood Road.

Group Size: The Reserve cannot accommodate large numbers at any one time.

Leaflets/Books/Guides: Descriptive Nature Trail Guide

Facilities

Catering: None.

Toilets: Available when car park open.

Shelter: Small Information Centre and viewing hides.

Disabled: One viewing hide available to disabled.

Amount of time taken: Nature trails 1 1/2-2 1/2 hrs.

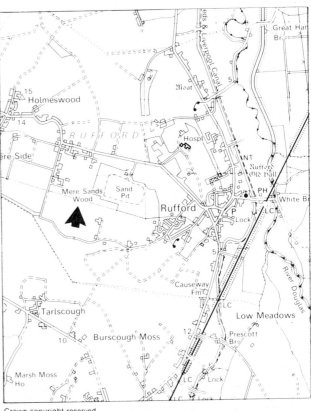

Crown copyright reserved

65

Pleasington Old Hall Wood Nature Reserve

The 14 acre site comprised a wooded valley infested with a dense understorey of rhododendrons and a derelict walled garden overgrown with rank vegetation and with 85% of its walls in ruin. Beginning in 1985, the rhododendrons were removed, footpaths laid and a bridge was constructed over the stream to provide access to the walled garden. Two hundred trees were planted in the cleared woodland areas, the garden wall was rebuilt and a pond and wetland area was started. Garden beds were sown with wildflowers and grasses. Various habitats have been created within the walled garden to cater for a wide range of species. Nine species of butterfly have been observed including Orange-tip, Small Tortoiseshell, Green-Veined White, Large White, Small White, Large Skipper, Small Copper and Meadow Brown. The newly created pond attracts much aquatic life-Damselfly and the golden Aeshna Dragonfly, frogs and toads. The woodland supports a variety of bird life including breeding Nuthatches and Lesser-spotted Woodpeckers. Five species of warblers may often be heard in the spring months. Rabbits and grey squirrels are numerous.

Open: All year.

Booking Requirements: Necessary weekdays for organised parties.

Admission Charges: Free.

How to get there 55

Address: Tourist Information Centre, Town Hall, Blackburn or Lancashire Trust for Nature Conservation, Cuerden Park Wildlife Centre, Shady Lane, Bamber Bridge, Preston PR5 6AU.

Contact: Peter Jepson. Tel:Blackburn (0254) 52201 ext.2067.

Location: The reserve is about 2 miles west of Blackburn town centre by Tower Road off the A674 Preston Old Road. It is adjacent to Witton Park and Pleasington Cemetery and Crematorium.

Ordnance Survey Grid Reference: SD 646 270.

Parking: Limited parking available within playing fields area.

Public Transport: Bus routes from Blackburn town centre.

Facilities.

Catering: Available at pavilion to playing fields.

Toilets: Available at pavilion to playing fields.

Shelter: No.

Disabled: Access to butterfly garden suitable for the disabled.

Amount of Time Taken: Depends on level of interest.

Group Size: Varies depending on interest. Contact Warden for advice.

Leaflets/Books/Guides: Yes.

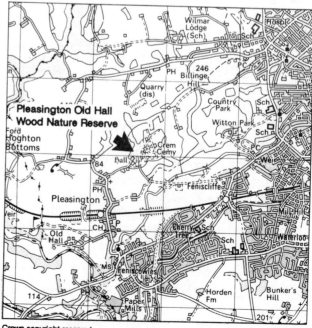

Crown copyright reserved

Warton Crag Nature Reserve

The Nature Reserve, which is an SSSI, is situated within the Arnside/Silverdale Area of Outstanding Natural Beauty. The Reserve is important both for its geological and wildlife interest. It exhibits typical carboniferous limestone land features, has a rich flora and provides a habitat for a variety of wildlife. The nature trail guide describes features of interest to be seen on a circular route of about 11/4 miles.

Open: Normally unrestricted opening.

*Booking Requirements:*Groups should arrange visits in advance.

Admission charges: Free.

How to get there 56

Address: Crag Road, Warton, Carnforth.

Contact: W.V.Crumley, City Architect and Planning Officer's Department, Palatine Hall, Dalton Square, Lancaster.
Telephone:Lancaster (0524) 39741.

Location: Warton, near Carnforth. M6 Junction 35 with A6, north of the junction signposted off A6. The Trail is located within Warton Crag Nature Reserve, on a limestone hill to the immediate west of Warton village. It commences from a car park in the old quarry above the Black Bull Hotel.

Ordnance Survey Grid Reference: SD 497 723.

Parking: Parish Council Car Park on Crag Road near to Black Bull Hotel, Warton.

Public Transport: Regular bus services to Warton village from Lancaster bus station.

Facilities

Catering: None. Village facilities.

Toilets: None.

Shelter: None.

Disabled: No special facilities. Terrain not generally suitable for wheelchairs.

Amount of time taken: One to two hours for full trail.

Group Size: It is recommended that only small groups visit the Reserve.

Leaflets/Books/Guides: Yes.

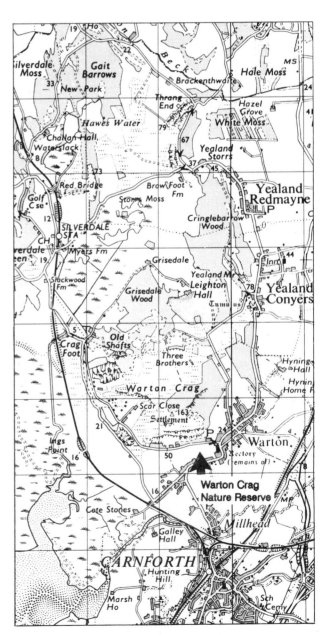

Crown copyright reserved

Please follow the Country Code:
Enjoy the countryside and respect its life and work.
Guard against all risk of fire.
Fasten all gates.
Keep your dogs under close control.
Keep to public paths across farmland.
Use gates and stiles to cross fences, hedges and walls.
Leave livestock, crops and machinery alone.
Take your litter home.
Help to keep all water clean.
Protect wildlife, plants and trees.
Take special care on country roads.
Make no unnecessary noise.

Town and Country Trails

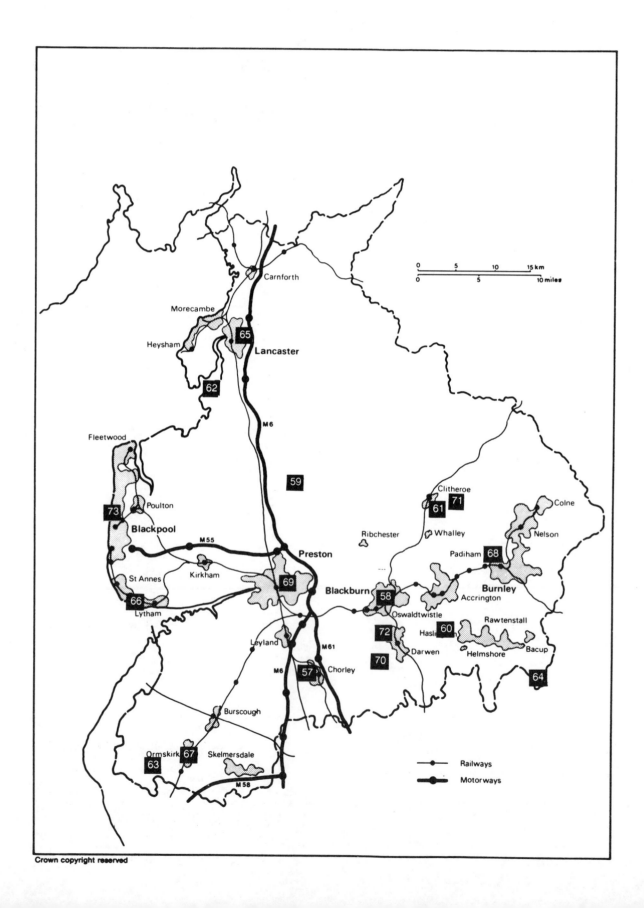

Carnforth

Morecambe

Heysham

65 Lancaster

62

M 6

Fleetwood

59

Clitheroe
61 71

Colne

73
Poulton

Blackpool

M 55

Ribchester

Whalley

Nelson

Padiham 68

St Annes
Kirkham

Preston

69

Blackburn
58

Burnley
Accrington

66
Lytham

Oswaldtwistle

Rawtenstall

Leyland

M 61

72
Hasli

60

Helmshore
Bacup

70
Darwen

M 6
57 Chorley

64

Burscough

Ormskirk 67
63
Skelmersdale

M 58

● Railways

● Motorways

Astley Park Nature Trail

The Nature Trail, which runs through Astley Park, was formerly waymarked but now remains merely as a distinct path through the woods. The walk has much to offer as a nature trail for those living in the Chorley area, but preliminary visits by a group organiser are advised. The main features of this Trail are the trees, the ground flora found under them and the birds to be seen in and around the area. The woods in Astley Park contain a great variety of English woodland trees introduced over many centuries. The walk commences at the paddling pool near the entrance gate and follows the path that crosses and recrosses the bridges over the River Chor. On the return journey from the bridge near Ackhurst Lodge, the left hand - northward path is taken and a visit can be made to the Hall and ornamental pond. The length of the Trail is about 1 3/4 miles in total.

How to get there 57

Location: Located in the grounds of Astley Park, the main entrance in Park Road, (A6), Chorley and is well signposted from all main roads in Chorley. Refer to the Astley Hall entry, page 3.

Ordnance Survey Grid Reference: SD 582 179.

Parking: Car park in Astley Park.

Public Transport: Start of Trail is near the main gate opposite Chorley bus station and less than half a mile from the railway station.

Facilities

Catering: Light refreshments available at the cafe, a converted coach house, next to the Hall. Extensive grass areas for picnicking with a number of picnic tables by the Hall.

Toilets: Toilet facilities are available in the coach house building adjacent to the Hall.

Leaflets/Books/Guides: Trail booklet available from Amenities Officer, Public Baths, Union Street, Chorley PR7 1AB.

Old Blackburn

The township of Blackburn dates from before the Norman Conquest. Until the 18th century it remained a little market town known chiefly for its cattle market and its woollen weaving. Great changes took place in the 18th and 19th centuries when cotton replaced wool as the major industry. Between 1800 and 1900 the population grew from 10,000 to 100,000. This Walk passes through areas which to a large extent reflect that period of development. The Walk begins and ends at the Lewis Textile Museum in Exchange Street.

How to get there 58

Location: Town centre of Blackburn. See the Lewis Textile Museum for details. The Trail is in a compact area of the town centre.

Leaflets/Books/Guides: An annotated guide to the Trail is available from Blackburn Museum and Art Gallery, Museum Street, Blackburn.

Fish Lane (Cardwell Place) in the last century

Brock Valley Nature Trail

The Trail is approximately 1 1/2miles long and follows a public footpath running down the Brock Valley from the car park at Lower Brock Mill to near the derelict Brock Bottom Mill and returns by the same route. The Valley is rich in woodland and aquatic plants and in birds of woodland and river. Fast following streams with their sources in high rainfaill areas lent themselves to the development of water power based industry. The industrial settlement dates from the 18th and early 19th centuries. There are many good examples of stream work and changing valley form, including meanders, terraces, and river cliffs.

How to get there 59

Address: Lancashire Trust for Nature Conservation, Cuerdon Park Wildlife Centre, Shady Lane, Bamber Bridge Bridge PR5 6AU.

Contact: LTNC. Telephone: Preston (0772) 324129

Location: The Trail is located about 1 mile west of Beacon Fell Country Park. From the M6 at Broughton Junction No.32, proceed north along the A6 for about 6miles then follow the AA signs to the Trail. From the east approach from Inglewhite or Beacon Fell. See the Beacon Fell Country Park entry.

Ordnance Survey Grid Reference: SD 543 430.

Parking: Car park at the start of the Trail but coaches cannot reach this, restricted width.

Facilities

None on site.

Amount of Time Taken: Up to 2 hours.

Leaflets/Books/Guides: From Lancashire Trust for Nature Conservation.

Calf Hey Trail

The air of desolation which still haunts Haslingden Grane makes the valley a fascinating area for walking. Calf Hey Trail is a short circular walk around Calf Hey Reservoir. For more than 70 years the Grane has been largely deserted and this Trail shows visitors something of how the place has changed during the last 500 years. Old hedgerows of rowan, oak and hawthorn and fragments of old woodlands are identified together with ancient trackways and ruined dwellings. A 17th century farmhouse abandoned before 1925 has been excavated to reveal the ground floor plan of the building.

Booking Requirements: Any formal event or activity in the area requires permission from the NWWA, enquire through the West Pennine Moors Information Service.

Contact: West Pennine Moors Information Service. Telephone:Horwich (0204) 691549.

How to get there 60

Location: Haslingden Grane is an area of moorland and reservoir scenery approximately 2 miles west of Haslingden, off the Grane Road, Haslingden to Blackburn B6232.

Parking: Calf Hey Car Park (off B6232); Clough Head Quarry Car Park (off B6232).

Ordnance Survey Grid Reference: SD 755 228 (Calf Hey) and SD 752 232 (Clough Head).

Public Transport: Bus route between Haslingden and Blackburn.

Facilities

Catering: None.

Toilets: None.

Shelter: None.

Disabled: Not suitable for disabled.

Amount of Time Taken: The Calf Hey Trail is approximately 1 1/2 miles long and will take about 1 hour to complete.

Leaflets/Books/Guides: Trail leaflet available from the West Pennine Moors Information Service, Rossendale Tourist Information Centre and Helmshore Textile Museum. There is an annual programme of guided walks, details from WPMIS.

Clitheroe Town Trail

Clitheroe is a market town of some considerable antiquity which still retains much of interest to the visitor. It is a most convenient place from which to explore some of the finest countryside in the north west, a large part of which is within the Bowland Area of Outstanding Natural Beauty. Interest in the town lies in the way that it has developed, with a heritage of mainly small but interesting buildings which reflect a history of continuous settlement from the 11th century onwards. Clitheroe originally developed from a cluster of buildings around the foot of the Norman Castle. The majority of the existing old buildings in the town centre date from the 18th and 19th centuries and much use is made in their construction of locally quarried limestone and sandstone. The old nucleus between the Castle and the Parish Church still retains its importance as the focal point of Clitheroe.

How to get there

Location: Clitheroe is situated to the north-east of Preston (15 miles), just off the A59 Preston to Gisburn road, between Pendle Hill and the Trough of Bowland, in the valley of the River Ribble.

Ordnance Survey Grid Reference: SD 740 415.

Parking: Car parking is available within easy walking distance of the Trail, on Station Road, Railway View and Lowergate. Free car parking maps available at Tourist Information Centre.

Public Transport: Buses stop in the town centre with services to Preston, Accrington, Blackburn, Burnley and Manchester and Skipton.

Contact: Tourist Information Centre. Tel:Clitheroe(0200)25566.

Address: Council Offices, Church Walk, Clitheroe.

Open: Monday to Friday 8.45am to 5.15pm Saturday/Sunday (Easter to end of October) 10am to 4pm.

Facilities

Food and Drink: There are several cafes, snack bars, restaurants and public houses serving bar lunches within Clitheroe. For details, contact the Tourist Information Centre.

Toilets: Available on York Street, Market , in the Castle grounds and at the Council Office car park.

Leaflets/Books/Guides: A Walk Through Clitheroe - published by the Ribble Valley Borough Council in association with the Clitheroe Civic Society - available from the Tourist Information Centre. This leaflet provides an illustrated guide to the town together with a map and a suggested route. The walk will take about one hour to complete.

Glasson Dock and Lune Estuary Nature Trail

The Trail follows a circular route along the coastal path on the south bank of the Lune Estuary along the line of a disused railway and returns on the Lancaster canal towpath. Glasson presents an interesting historical study since it is now a conservation area and many of the old buildings have been preserved. The Dock was opened in 1783 and was the port for Lancaster. Glasson is now used mainly for pleasure craft which moor in the canal basin but there continues to be commercial cargo operation with sea-going ships bringing grain and animal feedstuffs. It is possible to watch these ships being unloaded and also to watch the movement of ships and boats into and out of the port through the lock gates which are operated only at high tide. Many of the old houses for the dockworkers and the Customs House are completely unchanged and provide an attractive setting for the Dock.

How to get there 62

Address: Lancashire Trust for Nature Conservation, Cuerden Park Wildlife Centre, Shady Lane, Bamber-Bridge PR5 6AU.

Contact: LTNC.

Telephone: Preston (0772) 324129.

Location: The trail can be reached from Conder Green (A588 Lancaster to Cockerham) or from Glasson Dock (B5290 off A588).

Ordnance Survey Grid Reference: SD 448 560.

Parking: Public car parking at Conder Green and Glasson Dock.

Public transport: Bus service from Lancaster.

Facilities

Catering: Only those in the Glasson Dock area.

Toilets: At Glasson Dock.

Shelter: Not on the Trail.

Disabled: No special provision.

Crown copyright reserved

Haskayne Cutting

Ordnance Survey Grid Reference: SD 358 089.

Parking: None.

Public Transport: None.

Facilities

None on site.

Amount of Time Taken: About 1 1/2 hours.

Leaflets/Books/Guides: From Lancashire Trust for Nature Conservation.

Haskayne Cutting Nature Reserve and trail follows the route of a disused railway cutting in West Lancashire. It is surrounded by farmland and provides an important refuge for wildlife in this part of Lancashire. There are a wide variety of habitats, including areas of scrub, grassland, marsh and rock outcrops. Many interesting and attractive wild plants occur, notably marsh orchids and several plants more usually found along the coast or in the uplands. Over 60 kinds of birds have been seen. Outcrops of Keuper sandstone and core sections from a borehole provide interest for the geologists.

How to get there 63

Location: Situated about 3miles west of Ormskirk. From the Maghull-Southport road (A567) turn into Station Road at the Blue Bell Inn, Haskayne. The Trail is reached from the old railway bridge on Station Road, Barton.

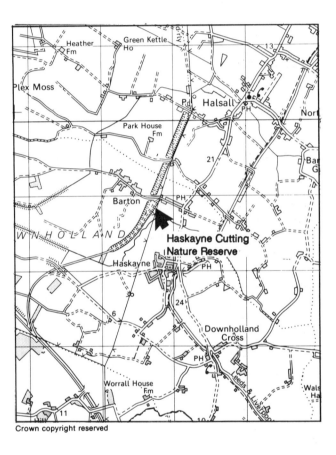

Crown copyright reserved

Healey Dell Nature Trail

The River Spodden has cut a winding steep sided valley to form one of the most important clough woodlands in the locality. It is in sharp contrast to the surrounding Pennine moorland and urban areas. Grassland and scrub alongside the river, part of the disused Rochdale-Bacup railway line (there is a magnificent stone viaduct), former mill lodges, and streams are all included in the Trail. Major features of historical significance are described. The clearly marked trail is suitable for all ages but suitable footwear should be worn.

Booking Requirements: Contact Warden for accompanied group visits.

How to get there 64

Address: The Visitor Centre, Healey Dell Nature Reserve, Healey Hall Mills, Shawclough, Rochdale OL12 6BG.

Contact: SarahWilson - Warden.
Telephone:Rochdale (0706) 350459.

Location: The Reserve lies in the lower Spodden Valley between Rochdale and Whitworth, some two miles to the north west of Rochdale town centre, and can be approached from the A671 at the junction of Market Street and Shawclough Road, Whitworth.

Ordnance Survey Grid Reference: SD 880 159.

Parking: At the Visitor Centre and at Broadley Wood Lodge, off StationRoad. Coaches by arrangement.

Facilities

Catering: None.

Toilets: When Visitor Centre is open.

Shelter: None.

Disabled: Not suitable.

Amount of Time Taken: 2hours.

Group Size: Guided tours limited to 40.

Leaflets/Books/Guides: Leaflets, walking guides and routes, maps.

The Railway Viaduct, Healey Dell

Lancaster Town Trail

The Town Trail follows a circular route around Lancaster examining the historical aspects of the City which dates from Roman times. The earliest known settlement was in the Castle Hill area where a Roman fort was built in 79 AD in order to command the crossing of the Lune by the Roman road from Chester to Hadrian's Wall. Excavations suggest there were five forts on this site, the last one used in part as a naval base to guard the coast against pirate raids across the Irish Sea. Very little is known about the site until Norman times but a Christian church was built in the 9th century and most of the inhabitants probably lived on Penny Street where the Roman road used to run.

The Castle was begun by Roger of Poitou in the 11th century but today only the Keep remains from this time. The nearby Priory Church was founded as a small monastery in 1094 but there have been no monks there since about 1430. This hilltop is an excellent vantage point to look down along the River Lune to St.George's Quay, many of the city's buildings and the medieval bridge. The canal and its associated cotton mills can also be seen along with the magnificent arched viaduct over the River Lune. The oldest group of houses is to be found around the base of the hill leading down to the city centre.

Towards the city centre several small alleyways, which were built as housing areas in the 18th century, can be explored and although today they are used as shops and offices many of the original buildings are still preserved. Towards the north of the city centre an area of Georgian houses can be seen close to the bus station. They were built with the prosperity brought by the port in the 18th century. St.George's Quay is now a quiet tree lined road but several of the old wooden warehouses still stand close to the old Customs House halfway along the Quay.

The shopping area of Lancaster is housed in a mixture of new development including a new shopping precinct and an area of preserved buildings. On the eastern side of the city, close to the canal, is a site which has been used by breweries for 200 years. The Cathedral of St.Peter can also be found in this part of the city, close to the Town Hall which stands facing the large monument to Queen Victoria.

How to get there 65

Location: The City of Lancaster is situated at the head of the estuary of the River Lune in the north of Lancashire. It has good lines of communication to all parts of the country via the M6 motorway. Junction 33 south and 34 north, and via the main London to Glasgow railway line.

Ordnance Survey Grid Reference: SD 472 618.

Guide Book: A Walk Around Historic Lancaster by John Champness available from local shops and from John Champness, 90 Aldcliffe Road, Lancaster.

Lytham and St.Annes Town Trails

The two halves of Lytham St.Annes developed in distinct and different ways. Lytham, referred to in the Domesday Book, had its origins as a fishing village perched at the end of an unbroken range of sandhills that ran northwards to Blackpool. Its development as a residential area and holiday resort received its greatest impetus with the coming of the railway in 1846, making it easily accessible to Preston and the rapidly expanding industrial towns of central and east Lancashire. However, the local 'Lords of the Manor', the Clifton family, kept close control over the general planning and their insistence on a high standard of development is reflected today in the qualities of the town centre buildings featured in the Town Trail. The township of St.Annes developed more dramatically from a plan by the then local land agent to the Clifton family, his son and a group of Rossendale businessmen. Imbued with the pioneering spirit of the 19th century they shared a vision to build a thriving garden city on the fringes of the Ribble Estuary. Lytham Common, lying between Lytham and Blackpool was chosen as the site and the St.Annes Land and Building Company was formed to undertake the development to a high standard comparable with neighbouring Lytham. Both the Lytham and the St.Annes Town Trails are designed by the Lytham St.Annes Civic Society to offer a greater awareness of the details of the urban environment and to provide some historical background to the buildings and features observed.

How to get there 66

Location: LythamSt.Annes is situated immediately to the south of Blackpool on the A584 (Blackpool-Preston road) which runs parallel to the coastline giving good access to the town.

Ordnance Survey Grid Reference: Lytham Town Centre - SD 366 272. St.Annes Town Centre - SD 320 288.

Parking: There is on-street parking on many of the streets in and around the town centre and a number of small car parks signposted in both centres.

Public Transport: Regular bus services operate in the town and there are services to Blackpool and Preston.

Contact: Tourist Information Centre, The Square, LythamSt.Annes (Summer only). Tel:St.Annes (0253) 725610. Tourist Information Centre, Town Hall, Lytham St.Annes. Tel:St.Annes (0253) 721222.

Facilities

Full range of town centre facilities. For details contact Tourist Information Centres.

Toilets: Available in both town centres and toilets with facilities for the disabled are available at The Monument, The Promenade, St.Annes and at The windmill, Lytham.

Leaflets/Books/Guides: Assorted leaflets and publications.

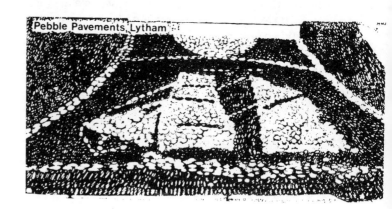
Pebble Pavements, Lytham

Ormskirk Town and Country Trails

The Trails present a vivid experience of this historic market town - a voyage of discovery bringing the past back to life, spanning the Dark Ages, Agincourt, the Civil War, 18th century elegance, 19th century squalor and present day Ormskirk where past and present live picturesquely side by side. There is a short trail, a long trail, and a combined town and country trail, ranging between about 45 minutes and two hours. The three trails inter-link.

How to get there 67

Town centre of Ormskirk, starting point of the short trail is the Parish Church.

Facilities: Town centre facilities.

Leaflets/Books/Guides: The Trails are not way-marked.The Trail Guide is available from Ormskirk Bookshop, 30 Burscough Street, Ormskirk.

Padiham Town Trail

A town trail booklet is published by the Burnley and District Civic Trust. The booklet contains a sketch map with the Trail through the town marked on it. The Trail is described and black and white photographs are included. However, the description is not separated into numbered observation points, thus when following the Trail it is advisable to have read the booklet thoroughly beforehand to appreciate it to its full. The book describes some of the buildings and smaller items which given Padiham its character, and gives something of their history anbd tries to capture something of the town's flavour.

Padiham existed well before the Norman Conquest. For centuries Padiham was a market town and the centre where produce from Pendleside was bought and sold. The town was sandwiched between the two great estates of the Shuttleworths of Gawthorpe Hall and the Starkies of Huntroyde. Both family seats can still be seen although they were considerably modified in Victorian times. The town was influenced greatly by the industrial revolution, factories grew up, terraced houses were built for the workers and rail lines linked Padiham with the rest of Britain. However, only the earlier more picturesque phase of the industrial Revolution affected the heart of the town. The hilly core of the town retains a street pattern character of those earlier days. Narrow and winding lanes cross at angles, cobbled alleyways run off into forgotten corners and even the main road is winding. It is all a great contrast to the rigid Victorian grid iron of streets laid out below. This central core has now been made a conservation area by Burnley Corporation.

How to get there 68

Location: The Trail starts at the Town Hall in Padiham. Padiham is situated on the A671 road between Whalley and Burnley. It is approximately 3 1/2 miles from Burnley and 8 miles from Blackburn via the A678.

Ordnance Survey Grid Reference: SD 794 338.

Public Transport: The town is well served by public transport with buses every few minutes to Burnley, Nelson and Colne. The nearest railway stations are at Burnley (Barracks) 2 miles. Rose Grove 1 3/4miles and Hapton 1mile which are served by the Preston-Colne local service.

Miscellaneous: The Trail is well signposted and follows mainly hard surfaced roads and paths, thus it is possible for persons in wheelchairs to follow it. However, some of the streets are fairly steep and some are cobbled and detours off the original Trail may be necessary.

Preston Town Trail

There is a leaflet "Preston Town Trail" prepared for Preston and South Ribble Civic Trust. Guides are availbale from The Tourist Information Centre, At Leisure Shop, Guild Hall Arcade, Lancaster Road, Preston PR1 1HT. Tel:(0772) 53731. The leaflet gives an annotated guide to the Trail and its main points of interest. It is designed to provide information and to stimulate thought on the character of Preston. A short bibliography is also included suggesting further sources of information on Preston.

Preston is an industrial town of some 120,000 inhabitants, situated at the lowest bridging point on the River Ribble. A "Guild Merchant" festival is held every 20 years to celebrate the trade and industry in the area. The town underwent great expansion during the industrial revolution due to its importance in the cotton industry. The walk is intended to show how the streets and squares hang together as a structure of spaces, which make up the town, rather than a set of individual buildings. It is intended that this will help to identify what makes up the special character of the place and help to form opinions and pinpoint the good and bad aspects of Preston as it stands today.

How to get there 69

Location: Starting point in Preston Market Place in the centre of the town off Lancaster Road at the end of Market Street. This is near to the Harris Library Museum and Art Gallery.

Ordnance Survey Grid Reference: SD 540 293.

Public Transport: Preston is served by good rail and bus links to all areas of Lancashire and is situated on the main railway line from London to Glasgow.

Parking: Multi storey car parks are adjacent to the Trail.

Roddlesworth Nature Trail

The Trail runs through the valley of the River Roddlesworth and covers several historic sites including the ruins of Hollinshead Hall, Garstang Hall and Hollinshead Cotton Mill, as well as Halliwell Fold Bridge. Rocky Brook, a local name for the River Roddlesworth, has been for many years a favourite place for picnics and walks. The Trail was created so that people could gain more satisfaction from their visit by observing some of the plants, birds and historic features described. It passes through woodland, follows the river valley and includes public footpaths on land owned by the North West Water Authority. There is a permanently marked orienteering course and maps are available.

Booking Requirements: Any formal event or activity within the area requires permission from NWWA. Enquire at West Pennine Moors Information Service.

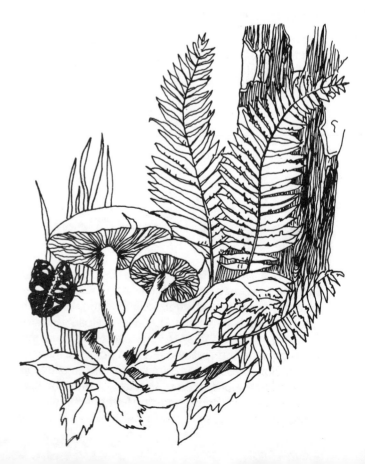

How to get there 70

Location: Trail starts from the Royal Arms Hotel, Tockholes. To enter the Trail walk alongside the railings away from the bus shelter and go through the gate opposite the car park. Take the path downhill to the left.

Parking: Adjoining the bus stop.

Public Transport: Local service to Tockholes.

Ordnance Survey Grid Reference: SD 665 216.

Facilities

Catering: At the Royal Arms Hotel during licensing hours.

Toilets: None.

Shelter: None.

Disabled: Not suitable.

Leaflets/Books/Guides: Trail guides and orienteering maps from Royal Arms Hotel, West Pennine Moors Information Service, and Tourist Information Centre, Blackburn.

Miscellaneous Information: The area is the property of the North West Water Authority and is in a drinking water catchment area. Observe the Country Code.

Salthill Quarry Geology Trail

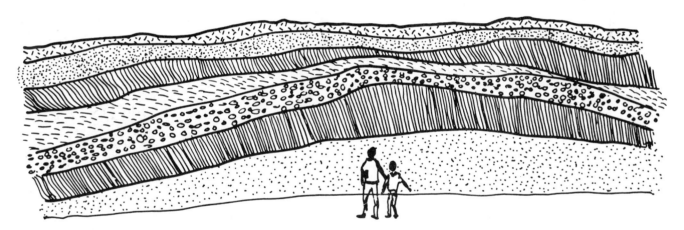

A leaflet and a booklet are available for use in conjunction with the Trail. The Salthill Geology Trail leaflet combines a map with general information and details of viewpoint positions around the Quarry. The booklet has more detailed information about the geology at specific points on the route around the Quarry. They are available from the Tourist Information Centre, Church Walk, Clitheroe. Tel:Clitheroe (0200) 25566.

The Trail has been constructed around a former disused limestone quarry on the outskirts of Clitheroe. Lime was once the main trade in Clitheroe and the site was originally quarried for limestone for building and industrial purposes. Since the beginning of this century the quarrying activity has slowly declined and eventually ceased. The Quarry has now been reclaimed for industrial use and the Geology Trail has been planned and constructed in conjunction with this. The Geology Trail is open at all times to the general public. The nearest available toilets are in Clitheroe town centre. Car parking is also available in Clitheroe but it is possible to park on the service road leading to the industrial estate although it should be emphasised that drivers should park so as not to cause any inconvenience to the users of the industrial estate. Several

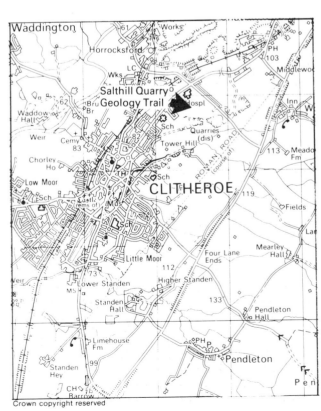

Crown copyright reserved

of the rock faces in the quarry are unstable and great care should be taken if approaching these particularly after frosty weather. Visitors should be encouraged to keep to the main footpath and not enter the fenced off areas since these are to protect the public from particularly unstable rock faces. The Quarry is a prolific source of fossils but it should be emphasised that the collecting of fossils and samples should be restricted for the benefit of future visitors since the supplies are not limitless.

How to get there 71

Location: The Quarry is situated to the north-east of Clitheroe. From the town centre travel along Chatburn Road then follow the Pimilico Link road and the new industrial estate service road. If approaching from outside the town the Quarry can be reached via the A59 Trunk Road, either going direct to the site or parking in Clitheroe and walking.

Ordnance Survey Grid Reference: SD 756 426.

Sunnyhurst Wood and Visitor Centre

The Wood covers about 50 acres extending down the valley of Earnsdale Brook to Hawkshaw. There are seven miles of footpaths. The Visitor Centre garden has name tags alongside each variety of wild plant which can be found in the Wood as well as garden plants. The Tree Trail is approximately 3 miles long, the route commences at the Cottage and follows the course of Sunnyhurst stream by the middle path. Towards the top western end of the valley the route veers to the south taking the top path on the southern edge of the wood to return to the Cottage. Prior to the early 1800's the area was farmland and, as with the farmland adjoining the Wood today, supported few trees. The first tree planting took place in the early 1800's, in an attempt to form a game reserve for sporting purposes. This early planting provides the area with the larger, older trees to be found today namely beech, oak, ash and elm - the basic trees of many older woods. Some hundred years later a second tree planting took place, when the area was developed as a public woodland park in the early 1900's. This later planting included the basic woodland tree species which had been planted in the early 1800's, but also included many other species namely, the purple and copper forms of beech, lime, alder, poplar, sycamore and chestnut of the taller broadleaved trees. Smaller broadleaved trees included mountain ash, whitebeam, birch, hawthorn, wild cherry, laburnum and holly. Conifers planted included Corsican pine, larch, spruce, cypress and yew. Since this large scale secondary planting only small scale plantings have occurred, the most evident being the planting of spruce, and the cherries and hawthorn in the 1960's. Alongside these plantings natural regeneration of trees from seed has occurred, namely, birch, oak, beech, holly, alder, willow, whitebeam and mountain ash. The result is a mixed woodland of various age groups which goes to make Sunnyhurst Wood an attractive and interesting area.

Opening Times: The Wood is open at all times, but the Visitor Centre is open only on Tuesday, Thursday, Saturday and Sunday and Bank Holidays Mondays, from 2pm to 4.30pm.

Admission Charges: Free.

How to get there 72

Address: Sunnyhurst Wood Visitor Centre, off Earnsdale Road, Darwen. Telephone: Darwen (0254) 71545.

Location: Turn into Earnsdale Road by the church, and there are three entrances into the Park along this road. Also leading off Blackburn Road adjacent to Earnsdale Road is Falcon Avenue with an entrance only about 50 yards from the main road.

Parking: Cars are not allowed in the Wood but there is adequate parking close to the three entrances in Earnsdale Road.

Public Transport: Railway station in Darwen town centre is just over a mile from the entrance to the Wood. Rail services operate between Blackburn and Bolton. There is a bus service along the A666 between Blackburn and Bolton.

Facilities

Catering: Kiosk and cafe, near the stream and Visitor Centre. There are many possible sites for picnicking in the Wood, especially at the shelter beyond the kiosk.

Shelter: A small shelter is located just past the kiosk near the stream.

Toilets: Visitor Centre when open and next to the kiosk, but the entrance is not suitable for wheelchairs.

Special Equipment Needed: Stout footwear and suitable protective clothing should be worn if the weather is bad.

Disabled: No special facilities for the disabled. There are steps down into the Wood from the lych gate entrances, but it may be possible to arrange for cars to enter the Wood and park by the Visitor Centre. Most of the paths along the Wood are broad and firm under foot.

Leaflets/Books/Guides: Guide to the Trees in Sunnyhurst Wood - John Firth. The Bird Life of Sunnyhurst Wood - David J.Pack.

Tram Heritage Trail

The Trail covers the stretch of sea front from Starr Gate in the South Shore area of Blackpool to the northern terminus of the tramway at Fleetwood. A leaflet explains the development of Blackpool along this route. The New South Promenade, opened in 1926, virtually doubled the length of Blackpool's Promenade. The Trail then passes the Pleasure Beach, Foxhall and the Golden Mile, the Golden Triangle bounded by the Winter Gardens, North and Central Piers; Talbot Square where Blackpool's first holiday hotels began, and on northwards through Cleveleys and Rossall to Fleetwood.

How to get there 73

The Trail is any part of Blackpool Promenade.

The Tram Heritage Trail leaflet is available from Blackpool Tourist Information Centres.

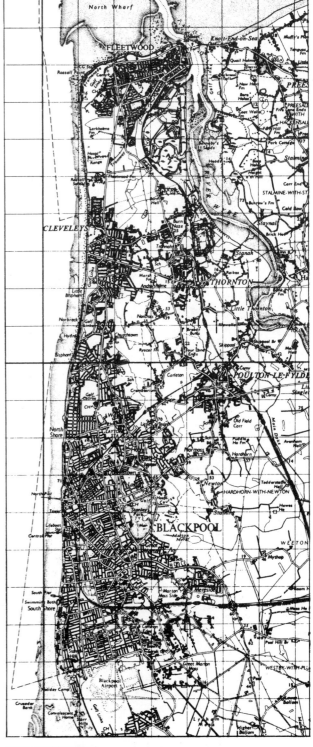

Crown copyright reserved

Canal Excursions

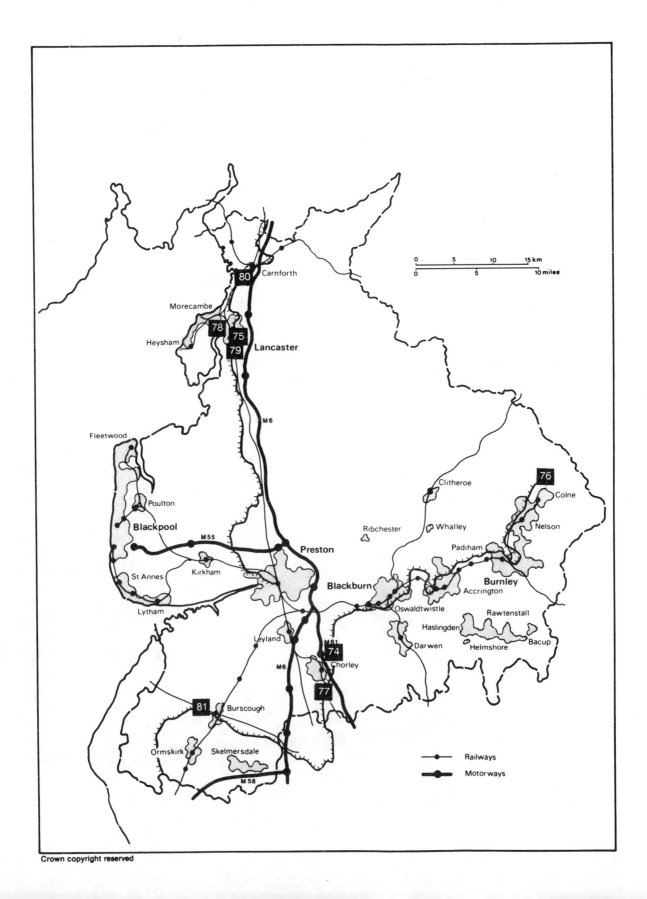

0 5 10 15 km
0 5 10 miles

Carnforth

Morecambe

Heysham

Lancaster

M6

Fleetwood

Clitheroe

Colne

Poulton

Ribchester

Whalley

Nelson

Blackpool

Padiham

M55

Kirkham

Preston

Burnley

St Annes

Accrington

Blackburn

Rawtenstall

Oswaldtwistle

Lytham

Haslingden

Bacup

Leyland

Darwen

Helmshore

M61

Chorley

M6

Burscough

Ormskirk

Skelmersdale

M58

Railways

Motorways

Boatel Cruises

Operate private party, educational and pleasure cruises on the Leeds-Liverpool Canal. Cruise itineraries include negotiating several locks and passing under a variety of bridges, representing various transport networks. The environmental surroundings vary from small industrial developments to both arable and pastoral farmland, and give an opportunity for sighting a selection of local wild life.

Throughout the cruise a commentary about the general history of the canals can be given. Both cruise and commentary can be adapted to supplement projects such as Canal Navigation, Modes of Transport, Canal Networks and Lock Operations, The Evolution of the Pleasure Craft Industry, Canal Industry, Canal Wildlife, etc.

Cruisers are fitted with large windows, giving ample viewing for all aboard; they are fully heated and ventilated according to the season.

Opening Times: Cruising every day all year round. Hire times according to prior arrangement.

Booking Requirements: Groups are advised to book well in advance. Confirmation of final numbers not later than 14 days prior to cruise.

Charges: Contact the booking office for details.

How to get there 74

Address: Boatel Party Cruises, The Boatyard, Kenyon Lane, Wheelton, Chorley PR6 8JD.

Contact: The Booking Office (Address above). Tel:Chorley (02572) 73269.

Location: "The Royal Sovereign", sailing from Top Lock, Wheelton.

Ordnance Survey Grid Reference: SD 597 214.

Situated off the A674 Chorley to Blackburn road about 3 miles from Chorley. Turn off the A674 at Wheelton on the left hand side of the road just past the "Red Cat" pub when approaching from Chorley, and on the right hand side just part the Heapey turn-off when coming from Blackburn. The sailing point is near the bridge crossing the Leeds-Liverpool Canal which leads out of Wheelton towards Whittle-le-Woods.

Parking: Ample car and coach parking space.

Public Transport: "The Sovereign"; Wheelton Top Lock, bus service from Blackburn to Chorley passing through Wheelton.

Facilities

Catering: Arrangements can be made for full dining facilities and for refreshments such as minerals, crisps, etc., to be on sale.

Toilets: Available on board.

Disabled: No special facilities for the disabled.

Average Length of Time Taken: Cruises for groups last about 4 hours.

Group Sizes: Minimum 40, Maximum 60.

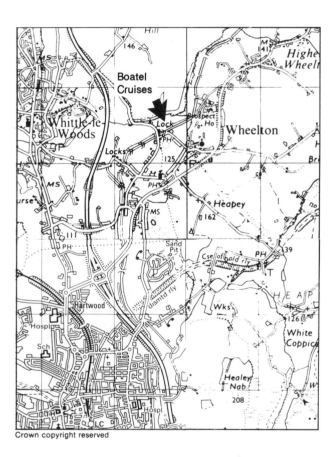

Crown copyright reserved

Canal Cruises - Duke Of Lancaster

Public and private cruises from the flower filled landscaped boatyard right in the city centre. Within minutes of embarkation the "Duke of Lancaster" is cruising through open countryside to the Lune Aqueduct, Glasson Dock, Garstang and other places of interest.

Opening Times: Cruises daily all year round but usually closed at some time during February.

Booking Requirements: Book in advance is advised.

Admission Charges: Hire charges.

How to get there 75

Address: Canal Cruises, Penny Street Bridge Wharf, Lancaster LA1 1XN.

Contact: Mr.C.Bennison.

Telephone: 0836-633189 (Cellnet).

Location: South side of Lancaster town centre. Adjacent to Royal Lancaster Infirmary on A6. Follow A6 north from Junction 33 on M6.

Ordnance Survey Grid Reference: SD 478 613.

Parking: Adjacent at Thurnham Street public car park.

Public Transport: Royal Infirmary bus stop.

Facilities

Catering: All day food, tea, coffee. All day bar.

Toilets: Yes.

Shelter: Yes.

Disabled: No special facilities.

Amount of Time Taken: Public cruises from 1 1/2 hours to all day. Private cruises average 4 hours. Youth weekend breaks (sleeping on the boat).

Group Size: 12.

Leaflets/Books/Guides: Yes.

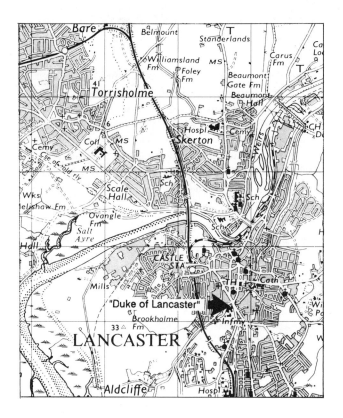

Foulridge Leisure Cruises

Several different cruises are available abroad the Marton Emperor, a 55ft long, 10ft.6in wide vessel with seating and table arrangements and opening cabin windows. Cruises on the Summit Pool start from Foulridge and move away from the industrial area into upland Pennine countryside with picturesque stone bridges and nearby old farms. Cruises on the Marton Pool cover the more remote parts of the Canal in upland moorland and through quiet villages. Cruises on the Burnley Pool travel through Nelson and Brierfield towards Burnley giving an insight into the industrial heritage of the area. Cruises in Burnley incorporate the Weavers Triangle, one of the best preserved industrial areas in the country. Passage through one of the lock systems is available on most cruises. Commentaries are available by arrangement when booking. Folk evening cruises are available to charter hire for parties; some open to the general public, all departing Foulridge Wharf. Short cruises open to the general public and departing Foulridge Wharf are available most days subject to charter hire.

Opening Times: April to October inclusive. Shop opens 9am-5.30.

Booking Requirements: Charter bookings for parties should be made well in advance. Public cruises may be booked by telephone on the day.

Charges: Details available on request.

How to get there 76

Address: Canal House, Warehouse Lane, Foulridge, Colne, Lancashire BB8 7PP.

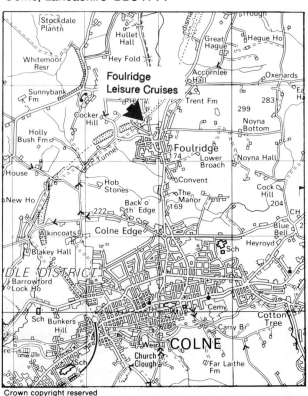

Crown copyright reserved

Disabled: No special provisions but disabled or handicapped welcome. Space for some wheelchairs and help to board.

Average Amount of Time Taken: Trips available from 1 1/4-8hours.

Group Size: Maximum number of passengers must not exceed 50 including supervisors. Folk evenings maximum 40 passengers.

Leaflets/Books/Guides: Yes on request.

Contact: Kevin Rollins,
Tel:Nelson (0282) 869159.

L and L Cruisers

L and L Cruisers of Heath Charnock near Chorley offer opportunities to travel on the Leeds and Liverpool Canal, one of the most beautiful waterways in the country. The most spectacular stretches can be cruised from the base on a week's trip in one of the fleet of ten super modern steel narrow boats. Alternatively, two self-steer day-boats "Daybreak "I" and "II" have recently been built and can double as twelve seater trip-boats. "Daybreak" will cruise over an eleven mile lock-free stretch between Wigan top lock and Johnson's Hillock bottom lock, passing through Haigh Hall Country Park, along the upper Douglas Valley through Arley Woods, Adlington and Chorley and past interesting canal-side public houses.

Admission Charges/Prices: A comprehensive price list for weekly cruises, or one-day trips on the self-steer "Daybreak" can be obtained on request.

Open: "Daybreak" is available all year round (subject to canal conditions). Week-long hire cruisers from Easter to late October.

Centre Open: Monday-Friday 8.30am - 12.30pm, 1.30pm - 5.30pm, Saturday (Easter-November) 8am - 5.30pm, Sunday by arrangement.

How to get there **77**

Location: Just to the north of Adlington, by the A6. Leave M6 at Junction 27, take A5209 to Standish, at T junction with A5106 turn left, after 3 1/4 miles turn right into Rawlinson Lane. Boatyard on left at junction with A6. From the M61 leave at junction 7 or 8 and follow A6 to just to the north of Adlington, close to the junction with the A673 to Bolton, Rawlinson Lane is on the left if travelling from Adlington (south) and on the right if travelling from Chorley (north).

Ordance Survey Grid Reference: SD 595 142.

Parking: Ample space, no charge.

Public Transport: The nearest railway station is at Adlington (3/4mile) or Chorley (2 miles), both of which are on the main London to Glasgow line. Buses pass along the A673 at frequent intervals between Manchester, Bolton, Adlington, Chorley and Preston, and stop just a short walk away from the boatyard.

Location: Foulridge Wharf, Warehouse Lane, Foulridge.

Ordnance Survey Grid Reference: SD 883 426.

Parking: Car/coach parking at the wharf.

Public Transport: Colne to Skipton bus services.

Facilities

Catering: Meals on board for private charters. Drinks, crisps, etc, always available whilst cruising. Shop on site.

Toilets: Available at the rear of the boat.

Contact: L and L Cruisers. Tel:Adlington (951) 480825 or, out of office house - Horwich (0204) 697078.

Address: Rawlinson Lane, Heath Charnock, Chorley PR7 4DE.

Facilities

Catering: The marina has a shop selling ice-cream and soft drinks. Picnics can be enjoyed along the canal-side.

Toilets: At the boatyard and on the boats.

Shelter : At the boatyard and on all boats.

Disabled: No special facilities but disabled are welcomed and every assistance given.

Average Length of Stay: This depends on the length of boat hire, from all day to weekly hire.

Group Size: No more than 12 persons can be carried on "Daybreak". Weekly cruisers have from 2 to 8 berths.

Leaflets/Books/Guides: Marina shop sells canal souvenirs.

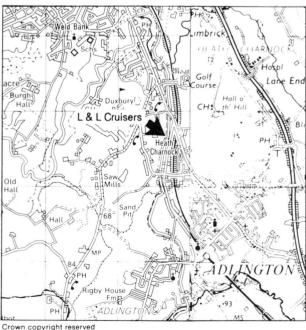

Crown copyright reserved

Lady Fiona Cruises

There are two cruises in opposite directions from Lancaster. One takes a route through the countryside towards Galgate and the other winds around the old parts of Lancaster and crosses the aqueduct over the River Lune. The excursion to Galgate takes approximately 3 hours and involves passing through woodland, agricultural and rural areas with views up to the Trough of Bowland. The tour around Lancaster is slightly shorter, taking appoximately 2 1/4hours and skirts the old parts of the town with views of the Castle and views up and down the River Lune. The Lady Fiona was originally a coal barge and then later a dredger on the Lancaster Canal. It is 72 feet long and 120 years old. The barge is 3 parts covered but has an open deck for viewing in fine weather.

Booking Requirements: Advance booking is required and confirmation is necessary to finalise numbers before the day of departure.

Charges: Available on request.

How to get there 78

Address: Lancaster Canal, Aldcliffe Road Basin, Lancaster.

Contact: Mr.T.Mitchell, 12 Westham Street, Lancaster LA1 3AU. Tel:Lancaster (0254) 39279.

Location: The canal basin at Aldcliffe Road is situated to the south of Lancaster city centre, approximately 200 yards from the A6. When approaching from the north leave the M6 at Junction 34 then follow Preston signs through the city centre and turn right at the Alexandra Hotel into Aldcliffe Road. From the south leave the motorway at Junction 33 and turn left after crossing the canal bridge.

Ordnance Survey Grid Reference: SD 477 612.

Parking: There is adequate free parking space adjacent to the canal bank for coaches, cars or minibuses.

Public Transport: Hourly bus services from Preston and Kendal to Lancaster city centre. The Canal is approximately a fifteen minute walk from the bus station and railway station. Rail access to and from Lancaster on the main line with routes to east and west Lancashire from Preston.

Facilities

Catering: There is a bar on the boat at which crisps and minerals are available for children. Food can be served on board the boat for private parties if this is booked well in advance. Cold buffets, hot pot lunch or supper.

Toilets: There are two toilets in cabins at the rear of the boat.

Disabled: Groups of disabled and handicapped people are welcome on the boat. A few steps have to be negotiated but there is plenty of space for wheelchairs.

Group Size: The boat is licensed for 75, but a maximum of 55 is recommended for comfort.

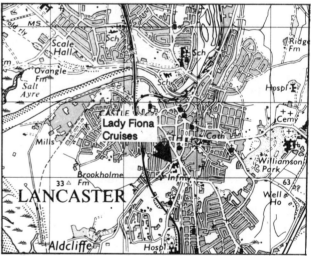

Crown copyright reserved

The Lancaster Packet

Evening pleasure cruise on the quiet Lancaster Canal on board a traditionally styled narrow boat. A five course meal is served in the heated restaurant and there is a fully licensed bar. The Lancaster Packet is available for individual table bookings or parties of up to 12 persons per cruise. Also, at Glasson Dock is the small craft "Hot Toddy" for short trips around the Dock and into the Canal branch, with other arrangements available on request.

Admission Charges/Prices: Charge includes trip and 5 course meal, details of which can be obtained on request.

Open: Cruising nightly from Easter to 31 October. Daytime trips by arrangement. Wednesday Boatman's lunch cruise 1.30-3.30pm.

How to get there 79

Location: The boat is moored opposite the Lancaster Royal Infirmary on the Canal at Aldcliffe Road in the centre of Lancaster.

Ordnance Survey Grid Reference: SD 475 612.

Parking: Free parking locally.

Public Transport: The Canal is about half a mile from Lancaster railway station and bus station and there is a frequent bus service along the nearby A6.

Contact: Mrs.W.Bowden. Tel:Lancaster (0524) 39291/39384.

Address: The Lancaster Packet, The Canal, Aldcliffe-Road, Lancaster or, 37 St.Oswald Street, Lancaster LA1 3AS.

Facilities

Food and Drink: The five course meal which is served in the heated restaurant is cooked aboard, and there is a fully licensed bar.

Toilets: On board.

Shelter: The narrow boat is fully enclosed against wet weather and heated throughout.

Facilities for the Disabled: Unable to accept wheelchairs.

Average Length of Stay: The evening trip commences at 7.30pm and lasts approximately 3 hours.

Group Size: Maximum of 12 persons per cruise.

Leaflets/Books/Guides: Yes.

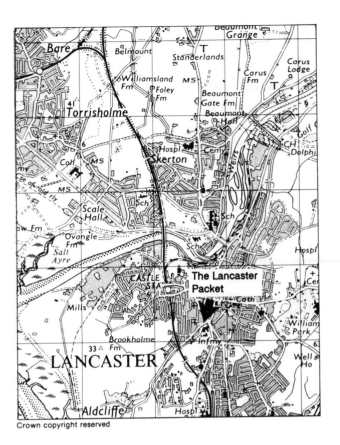

Crown copyright reserved

Nu-way Acorn

An opportunity to travel on the beautiful, peaceful Lancaster Canal in one of the fleet of self-drive day boats or selection of weekly hire craft from Nu-Way Marina, Carnforth. Visit historic Lancaster or small villages such as Galgate and Bilsborrow or travel to Glasson Dock, the Canal's only direct link with the sea. The waterway passes through some of Lancashire's most fascinating countryside and is of great historical and architectural interest.

Admission Charges/Price: Free admission to the marina. Comprehensive price list for vessel hire available on application. A discount for party bookings using more than one craft.

Booking Requirements: If a large party requires a boat prior notification must be given.

Open: Open all year for moorings and boat services, chandlery sales, etc. Day and weekly boat season from March to the end of October, operating time from 10am to 5pm.

How to get there **80**

Location: A6 from Preston or Lancaster, M6/A6 junction 35. At the traffic lights in the centre of Carnforth turn right if coming from the south, to the canal bridge traffic lights and then immediately right onto a track which leads past a football field to the marina.

Ordnance Survey Grid Reference: SD 497 702.

Parking: Ample free parking on both sides of the Canal.

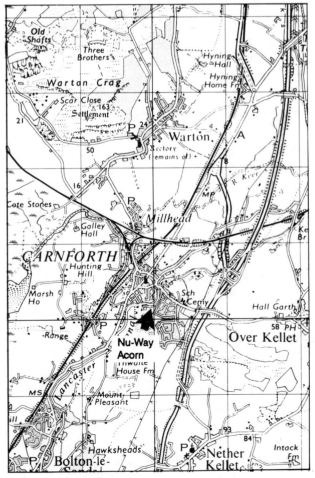

Crown copyright reserved

Public Transport: Nearest railway station at Carnforth (1/3mile) with regular services from Lancaster, Barrow and the north. There are regular bus services to Carnforth from Lancaster, Morecambe and Kendal

Contact: Nu-Way Acorn.
Tel:Carnforth (0524) 734457.

Address: Lundsfield, Carnforth.

Facitities

Food and Drink: No catering facilities.

Toilets: Yes.

Shelter: All the craft are covered with canopies.

Disabled: No special facilities but staff are available to give every assistance. A driver can be provided, at a small extra fee, for any party of disabled persons wishing to hire one of the self drive boats.

Average Length of Stay: Depends on length of boat hire from a few hours to all day or week.

Group Size: The maximum for any one craft is 10.

Leaflets/Books/Guides: Guide to the Lancaster Canal. Free leaflets on hire of weekly and day boats on request.

"Roland" Botel

Enjoy a leisurely Canal Cruise on board a comfortably converted former cargo-carrying boat along a stretch of once-thriving commercial waterway. Canal cruises have full meals or afternoon teas, and there are also school trips without meals which can include demonstrations of a lock and a dry dock.

Opening Times: Closed January and February and every Monday. Evening dinner cruises at 7.30pm, Sunday lunch cruises at 12.30pm, afternoon tea cruises by arrangement.

Booking Requirements: Advance booking for individuals and parties.

Charges: Available on request.

How to get there `81`

Address: The "Roland" Botel, Canal Wharf, Burscough, Ormskirk.

Contact: Frank or Margaret Boothby, Canal Cottage, Canal Wharf, Burscough, Ormskirk. Telephone:Burscough (0704) 894211.

Location: Behind the Admiral Lord Nelson public house at the canal bridge in Burscough on the A59 Liverpool to Preston Road.

Ordnance Survey Grid Reference: SD 443 121.

Parking: Public car park opposite the Admiral Lord Nelson.

Public Transport: Burscough is on the Manchester-Southport railway line and the Preston-Ormskirk-Liverpool bus routes.

Facilities

Catering: Full meals or light refreshments; fully licensed bars.

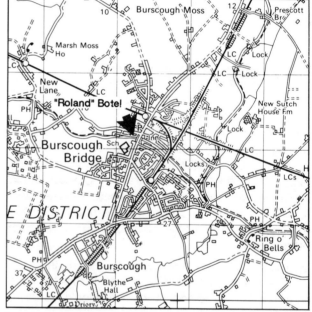
Crown copyright reserved

Toilets: On board.

Disabled: No special provision, but wheelchairs can be carried easily on board.

Average Length of Time Taken: Full meal cruises about 3-4 hours, afternoon cruises about 2 hours.

Group Size: Maximum number of passenger cannot exceed 56.

Leaflets/Books/Guides: Brochure on request.

Craft Centres

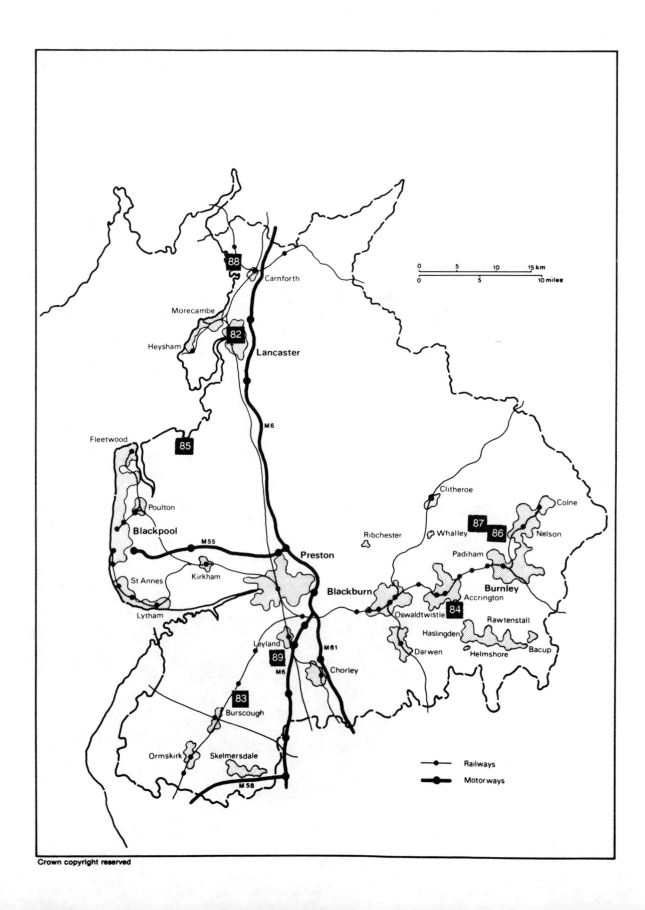

Carnforth

Morecambe

Heysham

Lancaster

M6

Fleetwood

Poulton

Blackpool

St Annes

Kirkham

Lytham

M55

Preston

Leyland

M61

Chorley

M6

Burscough

Ormskirk

Skelmersdale

M58

Clitheroe

Ribchester

Whalley

Colne

Nelson

Padiham

Burnley

Accrington

Oswaldtwistle

Blackburn

Rawtenstall

Haslingden

Darwen

Helmshore

Bacup

0   5   10   15 km
0   5   10 miles

Railways
Motorways

Crochet Design Centre

The only Crochet Design Centre in the UK. We produce a full-colour magazine, patterns, kits, etc. The only Diploma in Crochet is run from these premises. One-day courses and group talks available. All materials can be bought on the premises or through our mail order service.

Open: 9am - 5pm, Monday to Friday. Evening and weekend visitors can be catered for by special appointment.

Booking Requirements: Please ring or write for available dates.

Admission Charges: Free for casual callers. A charge is made for admission if organised talk/slide show/coffee is requested.

How to Get There 82

Address: White Cross, South Road, Lancaster LA1 4XH.

Contact: Rita Williams. Telephone:Lancaster (0524) 33309.

Location: Behind reception in the White Cross site facing Royal Lancaster Infirmary on the main A6 road into Lancaster from the south.

Ordnance Survey Grid Reference: SD 477 612.

Parking: On the sliproad and various car parks around the premises, public car park nearby.

Public Transport: Buses stop outside the door. British Rail approximately 1/4 mile away.

Facilities

Catering: Local facilities.

Toilets: Ladies on the ground floor (5steps). Gentlemen one floor up.

Shelter : Indoor establishment.

Disabled: Welcome although there is a limited space for wheelchairs, two at any one time is as much as can be catered for.

Amount of Time Taken: 3/4 - 1 1/2 hours depending on request of group.

Group Size: Up to one coachload of 56 people.

Leaflets/Books/Guides: Books on how to work all aspects of crochet; magazine; patterns etc.

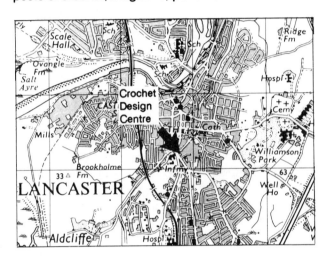

Eccles Farm Craft Centre

A Craft Complex with up to ten Craftspeople working and undertaking commissions. Lapidary, pottery, painting, needlework, cake decorating, bridal wear, woodcarving, bobbin lace making and toy making are amongst the crafts to be found here. There is a lecture room, weekend and day courses and training workshops are held. A shop sells goods produced on the premises and other local products. Eccles Farm Craft Centre won first prize in a 1988 national architectural competition to find the best conversion of a redundant farm building into a working unit offering tourism interest and jobs.

Opening Times: Daily except Monday, 10am-5pm but open on Bank Holiday Mondays.

Booking Requirements: Groups 12 + must book in advance.

Admission Charges: None.

How to get there 83

Address: Eccles Lane, Bispham Green, near Ormskirk L40 3SD.

Contact: Mrs.O.B.Burton. Tel:Parbold (02576) 3113 or 2075.

Location: Bispham Green is halfway between Parbold and Rufford off B5246.

Ordnance Survey Grid Reference: SD 487 129.

Parking: Yes. Coach parking restricted, prior arrangement necessary.

Public Transport: None.

Facilities

Catering: Light lunches, coffee, tea.

Toilets: Yes.

Shelter: Yes.

Disabled: Ramp entrance but no access to upstairs for wheelchairs. Toilet Facilities.

Amount of Time Taken: Dependant on level of interest in any individual craft.

Leaflets/Books/Guides: Leaflets available.

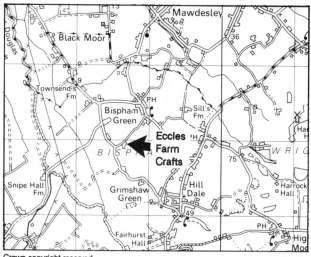

Crown copyright reserved

Holdings Country Pottery

The Pottery is situated in 35 acres of countryside on the edge of Oswaldtwistle Moors and dates from 1859. Holdings Country Pottery is a family concern dating from 1842. The present pottery was built to serve the needs of the local population, agriculture and industry. Local clay is still used and groups can see the complete clay process which includes hand making and firing. To gain the most from visits all groups have the services of an experienced guide. Presentation of information is varied to suit particular age groups and emphasis is given to geographical considerations and historical background. Normally all groups can see pottery being hand thrown.

Opening Times: Most weekends through the year. Weekday afternoons March to December and mornings in June to August. Evening tours are also available for groups.

Booking Requirements: All group visits must be booked in advance. Telephone for booking form.

Admission Charges: A charge is made for admission.

How to get there 84

Address: The Potteries, Oswaldtwistle, Lancashire BB5 3RP.

Contact: Tel.Accrington (0254) 32994 (day) Accrington 397055 (evening).

Location: The Pottery is on the A677 road, 4 miles from Blackburn and 4 miles from Haslingden.

Ordnance Survey Grid Reference: SD 732 257.

Parking: Large parking area for cars and coaches.

Public Transport: Blackburn to Accrington bus within 15 minutes walk.

Facilities

Catering: Coffee shop. The Pottery has a large picnic area, situated on the site of the original coal fired pottery kiln.

Toilets: Yes.

Shelter: Tours are for the most part indoors.

Disabled: Blind and disabled visitors can be accommodated if accompanied. The Pottery does not have disabled persons toilet facilities.

Average Length of Time Taken: Tours take approximately 40-60 minutes.

Group Sizes: From 25-55 plus.

Miscellaneous: In addition to manufacturing, Holding Bros. supply a wide range of craft materials. Worksheets relating to the Pottery are available.

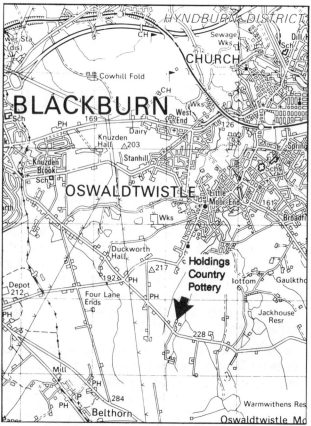

Crown copyright reserved

Pilling Pottery

This is a large studio Pottery producing a wide range of hand-thrown pottery in wholesale quantities. The Craft Shop stocks a wide range of hand made pottery, including garden pottery. The Shop is divided from the workshop by a glass partition so visitors can watch work in progress. Pottery equipment stocked and manufactured and this small family firm is in the forefront of development in high efficiency low thermal mass kilns. Potters wheels are sold which are ideal for the hobby potter or for tough use in schools, colleges and in production studio potteries. Special evening demonstrations by arrangement.

Admission Charges: None. Small charge per person for evening demonstrations.

Open: All year - Monday-Friday 9am-12.30pm, 1.30pm-5pm, Sunday 1.30pm-5pm. Please telephone to check whether the person best able to help you is on duty that day.

Booking Requirements: Parties and coaches should notify in advance.

How to get there ▧85

Address: Pilling Pottery, School Lane, Pilling, Near Preston, Lancashire.

Contact: Jim Cross. Tel:(0253) 790 307

Location: Pilling is a small village on the coast between the Wyre and Lune estuaries, to the west of the M6/A6, and to the north of Preston. Directions from M6 going north. Exit at Junction 32 and go north on A6, by-passing Garstang. Turn left directly after the Chequered Flag (large pub on left). One mile on, turn right into Killcrash Lane and follow for several miles to T junction at National Westminster Bank. Turn right here and continue to the first turn left, continue past windmill and turn left again. Follow road round past Church and Olde Ship Restaurant on right. The Pottery is the third house on the right past the Olde Ship. (Approximately 18 miles from M6). Directions from M6 going south. Exit at Junction 33. Head south on A6 towards Garstang and after approximately 1 mile turn right (on a long straight section of road) for Cockerham and Glasson Dock. Continue over a humped back canal bridge. Turn right at next T junction then left at the next T juncion. Continue downhill and along the shore for sev-

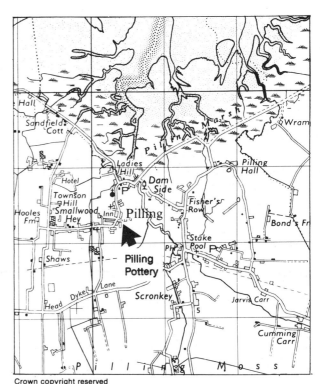

Crown copyright reserved

eral miles. When the road turns sharply left inland take the road to the right (directly after sign for Pilling Pottery). Continue straight over next T junction and then follow the road round past Church and Olde Ship Restaurant on right as above. (Approximately 7 miles from M6).

Ordnance Survey Grid Reference: SD 400 482.

Parking: Large car park in front of the shop will also take a coach.

Public Transport: There are services from Garstang, Knott End and Lancaster.

Facilities

Catering: None, but there are facilities in the village, an attractive picnic area on the beach at Fluke Hall, and a children's play area near the Pottery.

Toilets: Public toilets opposite the Pottery.

Disabled: The workshop and shop are all on the ground floor. Wheelchairs can be accommodated.

Amount of Time Taken: About 60 minutes. Evening demonstrations last about 45 minutes.

Group Size: For special demonstration, minimum 25, maximum 50-60.

Slate Age

This is a craft workshop producing a range of items for the gift industry but also undertaking a wide range of other work and commissions. The gift-products include clocks, barometers, lamps, vases, cutlery, bookends as well as business promotional gifts, all in polished or rustic finished slate. Raw materials and finished parts to customers own requirements are supplied to the trade and for DIY and this aspect includes such things as garden features, patios and fireplaces.

On arriving at Slate Age the visitor will be shown round the workshop where cutting and drilling uses diamond-tipped machinery. The polishing, bevelling and finishing takes place in the assembly workshop and visitors are able to visit the showroom if they so wish.

Admission Charges: None.

Open: All year, except Easter and Christmas. Please give 2/3 weeks notification for group visits.

How to get there 86

Location: Off the A6068 (Padiham-Nelson By-Pass) in north-east Lancashire, near Pendle Hill.

Ordnance Survey Grid Reference: SD 826 371.

Parking: On quiet lanes nearby.

Public Transport: On Ribble Service No.238 from Burnley to Blacko and on Ribble Service No.63/65 from Nelson. No Sunday service.

Contact: Mr.P.Rawlinson, Slate Age (Fence)Ltd. Tel:Nelson (0282) 66952.

Address: Fence Gate, Fence, Burnley BB12 9EG.

Facilities

Food and Drink: In public houses nearby.

Toilets: Available.

Shelter: Covered workshops.

Disabled: There are no steps.

Average Length of Stay: Up to one hour.

Group Size: Maximum 10 persons.

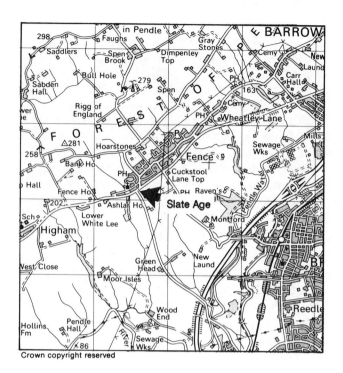

Crown copyright reserved

Trapp Forge

Trapp Forge is a well established family concern with an international reputation. Casual visitors will always find someone at the Forge but will have to take a chance on the type of work in progress. Most Sundays there is forging from 2-4pm. Groups (20-40) can book an evening visit when they will hear some of the history of ironwork, watch red-hot iron being forged, see a slide presentation, ask any questions and then browse in the "Aladdin's Cave" Showroom with forged iron, cast and malleable iron and many other metallic objects, antique and modern.

Admission Charges: None for individuals, nominal charge for group visits to demonstrations. Details on request.

Open: Daily 10am-5pm except Christmas Day and Boxing Day.

Booking Requirements: Groups should book well in advance.

How to get there 87

Address: Trapp Forge, Simonstone, Burnley BB12 7QW.

Contact: Mrs.Sheila Carter. Tel:Padiham (0282) 71025.

Location: Set in beautiful countryside in north east Lancashire, near Pendle Hill and Burnley. At Simonstone cross-roads on A671 Whalley to Padiham road, take the lane to Sabden for approximately 1/2 mile, go through the minor crossroads and Trapp Forge is the first drive on the left.

Ordnance Survey Grid Reference: SD 778 356.

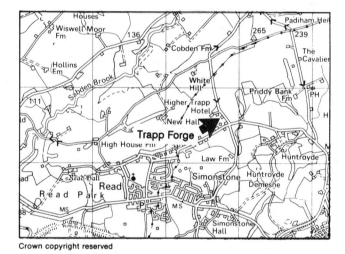

Crown copyright reserved

Parking: Ample free parking, coach parking is limited.

Public Transport: An infrequent service from Burnley to Clitheroe via Sabden, Ribble No.237.

Facilities

Catering: Several public houses nearby.

Toilets: None.

Shelter: Indoor workshop and showroom.

Disabled: Space is limited in the workshops and showroom, but visitors in wheelchairs would be able to enjoy the outdoor demonstrations on Sundays, 2-4pm.

Average Length of Stay: About one hour. Group visits rather longer.

Group Size: About 20 visitors in the workshop, up to 40 for outside demonstrations and slide-talk.

Leaflets/Books/Guides: A leaflet is available.

Wolf House Gallery

A gallery situated deep in wooded countryside with a unique selection of quality crafts for sale, such as hand-blown glass, pottery, woodcarvings, traditional wooden toys, rocking horses and sculpture. Many original paintings, mainly by professional artists, are also on sale. The Gallery is housed in carefully restored early Georgian farm buildings. Many of the original features have been incorporated in the excellent displays. There is also a studio, with panoramic views over the Kent estuary to the Lakeland Hills, where in the summer months art and craft subjects are taught to small groups of students. There is a textile gallery specialising in designer knitwear and hand-woven jackets and cloaks. The Gallery is one of few to have been selected by the Craft Council for its regional significance.

How to get there 88

Location: Near Jenny Brown's Point, Gibraltar, 12 miles north west of Lancaster, 12 miles south west of Kendal, ten minutes drive from the M6 (Junction 35) following signs for Silverdale.

Ordnance Survey Grid Reference: SD 460 740.

Parking: Ample facilities for private cars. No coaches during the daytime.

Public Transport: The nearest station is at Silverdale (1 mile) with trains from Lancaster. The Lancaster-Carnforth-Arnside-Kendal bus passes through Silverdale village (1/2 mile away), no Sunday service.

Contact: Edward and Denise Dowbiggin. Tel:Silverdale (0524) 701405.

Address: Wolf House Gallery, Gibraltar, Silverdale, via Carnforth, Lancaster LA5 0TX.

Facilities

Food and Drink: Small tea-room, no meals.

Toilets: Available.

Disabled: Individual wheelchairs can be accommodated.

Average Length of Stay: About 1-2 hours.

Group Size: Maximum number 40. Large groups by appointment.

Admission Charges: None.

Open: New Year to Easter - Saturday and Sunday only. 10.30am to 5.30pm; Easter to June - Tuesday to Friday 2pm to 5.30pm. Saturday and Sunday 10.30am to 5.30pm, closed Monday. June to mid-September - 6 days a week 10.30am to 1.pm, 2pm to 5.30pm, closed Monday. Mid-September to Christmas - Tuesday to Friday 2pm to 5.30pm Saturday and Sunday 10.30am to 5.30pm, closed Monday. (Open every Saturday and Sunday throughout the year).

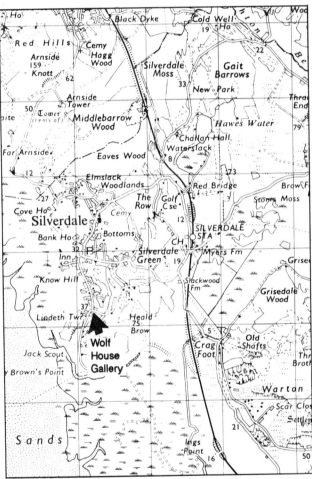

Crown copyright reserved

Worden Park Arts and Crafts Centre

The Worden Arts and Crafts Centre is in Worden Park which includes 160acres of open space and facilities include walks, a garden for the blind, arboretum, picnic area and a miniature railway (Sundays only). Adjoining Worden hall are the Crafts Centre and Arts Centre (the Marsden Room Theatre). Traditional crafts include blacksmith, enamelling, wood turning and pottery. The Arts Centre provides for exhibitions, visual and performing arts. Worden Hall, which is centrally located in the Park, accommodates in the Derby Wing the Lancashire Branch of the Council for the Protection of Rural England. Its facilities include a Visitor Centre with sales, information and exhibitions, and a Resource Centre which can be used by appointment. All the buildings are Grade II listed, and have been carefully restored.

Opening Times: Park-daily, sunrise to sunset. Visitor Centre - February to Easter Wednesday to Sunday 12-4pm; Easter to November Tuesday to Sunday 11am-5pm; December Wednesday to Sunday 12-4pm depending on weather conditions. Crafts Centre open all year, craftsmen in Tuesday to Sunday.

Booking Requirements: Minimum of 30 up to 100, book in advance.

How to get there 89

Address: Worden Park, Leyland PR5 2DJ.

Contact: The Manager, Worden Arts and Crafts Centre. Telephone: Leyland (0772) 455908.

Location: Situated on the south side of Leyland.

From Preston, Blackburn and Burnley, via M6 to Junction 28, take A49 Wigan road heading south. Take B5248 Heald House Road, signposted for Leyland and at Leyland Cross follow the signposts for Worden Park. From Southport, Liverpool and Ormskirk, northwards on A59 turning on the A581 for Croston then B5253 for Leyland. At Leyland Cross follow the signposts for the Park.

Ordnance Survey Grid Reference: SD 538 209.

Parking: Adequate facilities off Worden Lane. Smaller facilities at the Arts Centre. Coach parking by arrangement.

Public Transport: British Rail stations at Preston and Leyland with regular bus service from these to Leyland Cross.

Facilities

Catering: Coffee shop and snacks at the Craft Centre, open daily.

Toilets: Toilets available in the Park and at the Arts Centre.

Shelter: Visitor Centre and Craft Shops.

Disabled: Ramped access to Arts Centre and Craft Units.

Amount of Time Taken: Up to a whole day.

Leaflets/Books/Guides: Various guides, trail guides, at the Visitor Centre.

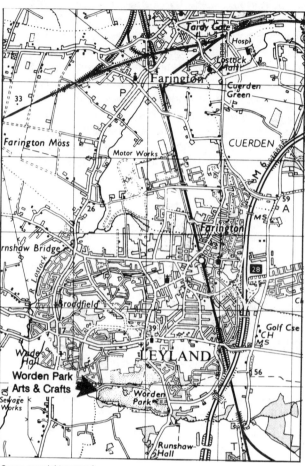

Crown copyright reserved

Industrial Visits

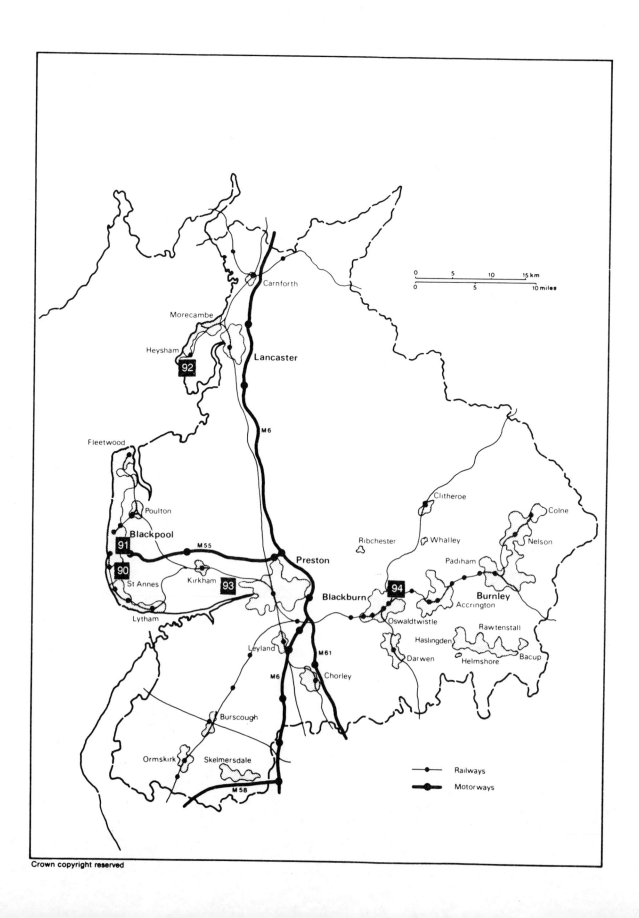

Railways

Motorways

Blackpool Airport

One of the best equipped small airports in Europe. Blackpool has 3 runways able to handle up to 737s/DC9s. Principal terminal for IoM and other Irish Sea routes. Busiest light aviation airport in the country. Fully licensed Air Traffic Control staff and the latest rescue and fire-fighting equipment provided to the CAA Category 6 standard for public licensed aerodromes. Full Customs and immigration and security service. Full ramp landing service for luggage and freight and refuelling for both jet and piston engine aircraft. On site heliport serves the Morecambe Bay gas rigs with regular helicopter flights.

Opening Times: 9am-9pm (summer), 9am-5pm (winter). These opening times refer only to arranging visits and are not the operational hours of the Airport. Visits are available seven days a week. No visits during July and August. Visits may be limited due to the operational demands of the airport.

Booking Requirements: Advance booking is essential in the case of guided tours, but not if just visiting the Public Enclosure. No young children on guided tours.

Admission Charges: No charge.

How to get there 90

Address: Blackpool Airport, Blackpool FY4 2QS.

Contact: Tel:Blackpool (0253) 43061.

Location: Situated on the southern boundary of the town about 2 1/2 miles from the town centre and on the northern boundary of Lytham St.Annes. The M55 motorway comes to within 4 miles of the Airport.

Ordnance Survey Grid Reference: SD 319 313.

Parking: Public car park.

Public Transport: The Airport has its own bus terminus for a route to the centre of Blackpool and the Inter-City station at Blackpool North, and buses for Lytham St.Annes run past the main gate. The rail link is from Preston, trains on the Blackpool South line stop at Squires Gate Station, 5 minutes walk from the Airport entrance. Blackpool Airport is also only 1/2 mile from the southern terminus of the tramway system running along the seafront from Starr Gate to Fleetwood.

Facilities

Catering: Buffet in Terminal Building.

Toilets: In Terminal Building.

Shelter: Most of the places visited are indoors.

Disabled: Toilets for the disabled in the Terminal building. All Terminal facilities are on one level.

Group Sizes: Parties limited to 25 in number, but larger groups can be divided to be taken round separately.

Leaflets/Books/Guides: Yes.

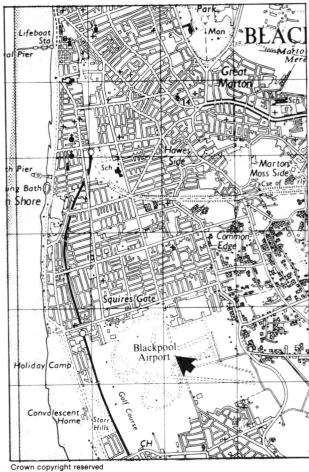

Crown copyright reserved

Coronation Rock

At Coronation Rock Company we can offer you the opportunity to watch from our visitor viewing gallery the fascinating skills of our sugar confectioners as they make lettered rock and other specialities such as sugar fruits. After viewing you have the opportunity to buy our products in our factory shop.

Opening Times: Monday to Thursday 9.30am-3pm, Friday 9.30am-2.30pm. Closed Saturday, Sunday and public holidays.

Booking Requirements: Yes, for group visits.

Admission Charges: Free.

How to get there 91

Address: Coronation Rock Co.Ltd., 11 Cherry Tree Road North, Marton, Blackpool FY4 4NY.

Contact: Mrs.M. Bell/Miss N.Robson.
Tel: Blackpool (0253) 62366/7.

Location: Just off A583 at the Evening Gazette office building on Preston New Road leading into Blackpool from M55.

Ordnance Survey Grid Reference: SD 336 345.

Parking: Yes.

Public Transport: Bus services from Blackpool town centre.

Facilities

Catering: None.

Toilets: Yes.

Shelter: Yes.

Disabled: Yes.

Amount of Time Taken: 3/4 hour.

Group Size: Up to 40.

Crown copyright reserved

Heysham Nuclear Power Station

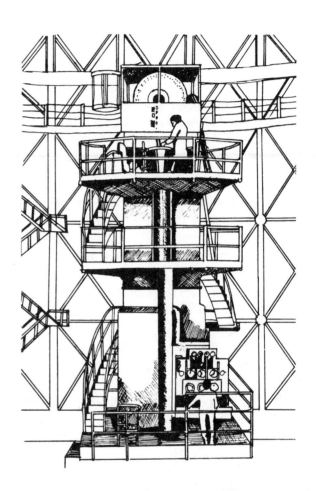

Heysham 1 Nuclear Power Station is one of the newest and most advanced in the country. A second station, Heysham 2, is being built alongside and will begin to generate electricity during 1988. An introductory presentation at the Power Station is followed by a tour, taking in all aspects of the process of producing electricity by nuclear fission. Visitors tour the turbine hall, see the reactors from a viewing gallery and also see the Central Control Room and Computer Room. A new display area is to be introduced during 1988.

Opening Times: Visits are available each weekday morning, afternoon or evening.

Booking Requirements: Tours are available by prior arrangement only and at least two weeks notice must be given.

Admission Charges: None.

How to get there 92

Address: CEGB, Generating Division, PO Box 4, Heysham, Morecambe LA3 2XQ.

Contact: Visits Organiser. Tel:Heysham (0524) 53131.

Location: Situated adjacent to Heysham Harbour off the A589 Heysham to Lancaster road. Leave M6 at Junction 34 then follow signs first to Morecambe and then Heysham Harbour.

Ordnance Survey Grid Reference: SD 400 598.

Parking: Car and coach parking available on the site.

Public Transport: Train to Morecambe station then bus to Heysham. Bus service hourly from Lancaster to Heysham.

Facilities

Catering: None.

Toilets: Available on the site

Shelter: The majority of the tour takes place indoors.

Amount of Time Taken: 2-2 1/2 hours.

Group Size: Maximum 30-35, likely to be increased to 50 during 1988.

Leaflets/Books/Guides: A number of publications are available from:- CEGB, Sudbury House, 15 Newgate Street, London EC1A 7AU. CEGB, Europa House, Bird Hall Lane, Cheadle Heath, Stockport SK3 0XA.

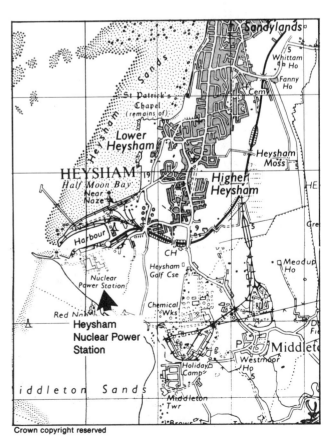

Crown copyright reserved

Springfields

Springfields is the largest self-contained nuclear fuel production plant in the world. Nuclear fuel elements are manufactured from uranium ore concentrate and over six million elements have been manufactured for home and overseas markets; the Queen's Award for Export was won in 1980. An introductory lecture is followed by a tour which shows the complete conversion of the uranium powder into fuel elements for nuclear power stations.

Opening Times: Visits can be made each weekday morning, afternoon and evening.

Booking Requirements: Tours are available by prior arrangement only and at least four weeks notice is required.

Admission Charges: Free.

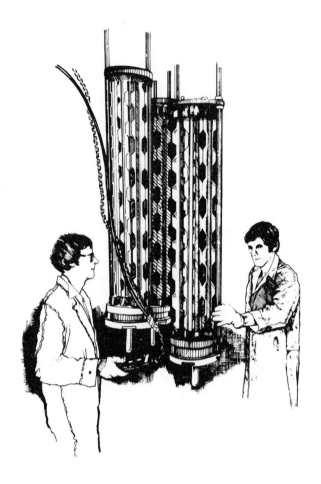

How to get there 93

Address: British Nuclear Fuels plc, Springfields Works, Salwick, Preston PR4 0XJ.

Contact: Information Services. Telephone: Preston (0772) 728262, ext 4576/4198.

Location: Approximately five miles west of Preston, north of the A583 Preston to Blackpool road. Leave M6 at Junction 32, and M55 at the linked Junction 1, bear left onto A6 for Preston and right on the A5085/A583 for Blackpool. On A583 turn right for Clifton.

Ordnance Survey Grid Reference: SD 464 315.

Parking: Car and coach parking on site.

Public Transport: Nearest main line railway station is Preston. Frequent Ribble bus services between Preston and Blackpool, alight at Clifton Village which is half a mile from the Main Gate.

Facilities

Catering: None. Light refreshments are supplied at the end of the tour.

Toilets: On site.

Shelter: Majority of the tour takes place indoors.

Disabled: Unable to accept disabled visitors due to stairs.

Average Length of Time Taken: Half a day.

Group Size: Maximum 25-30.

Special Provisions: Springfields is an industrial complex and sensible shoes must be worn.

Leaflets/Books/Guides: Yes.

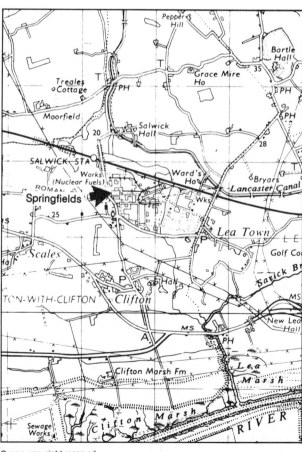

Crown copyright reserved

Thwaites Star Brewery

In 1807, around the time Napolean was busily declaring Britain to be in a state of seige, Daniel Thwaites set about brewing his own beer. Whether these two events were related is a matter for conjecture. Part of the original brewery still remains on the present site, alongside the new brewhouse and bottling plant. The new brewery, amongst the most modern in Europe, is almost totally given over to the production of real beer.

As well as pride in their beers, Thwaites have a deep affection for their Shire horses. These huge Shires are working horses but they are probably best known for their appearances at shows and carnivals.

A visitor to the Star Brewery is given an insight into the brewery process, visits the Company Museum and arrangements can be made for a visit to the stables.

Opening Times: Visits are available during working hours on Monday, Tuesday, Wednesday, Thursday and on Monday, Tuesday and Thursday evenings.

Booking Requirements: All visits by prior arrangement. Visits to the stables must be specifically requested.

Admission Charges: None. The Company suggests a contribution to its Guide Dogs for the Blind Appeal.

How to get there ▪94

Address: Daniel Thwaites plc, POBox 50, Star Brewery, Blackburn BB1 5BU.

Contact: Mrs.Avril Haworth. Tel:Blackburn (0254) 54431.

Location: Major town centre site. Entrance on Penny Street, A666 to Whalley, and accessible from Eanam, the A677 to Accrington.

Ordnance Survey Grid Reference: SD 685 282.

Parking: Available.

Public Transport: Within walking distance of all facilities.

Facilities

Catering: None on site. Advance bookings can be made for meals and drinks at the "Daniels" public house adjacent to the Brewery. Telephone: Blackburn (0254) 54997.

Toilets: Available.

Average Length of Time Taken: 1 1/2 hours.

Disabled: No parties of elderly people because of the strenuous nature of the visit. There are staircases to be climbed.

Special Provisions: Ladies are advised to wear flat shoes. There is no smoking within the Complex.

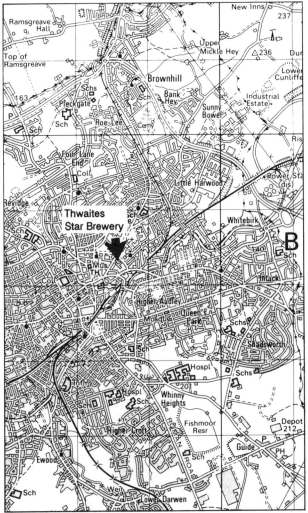

Crown copyright reserved

Leisure Parks

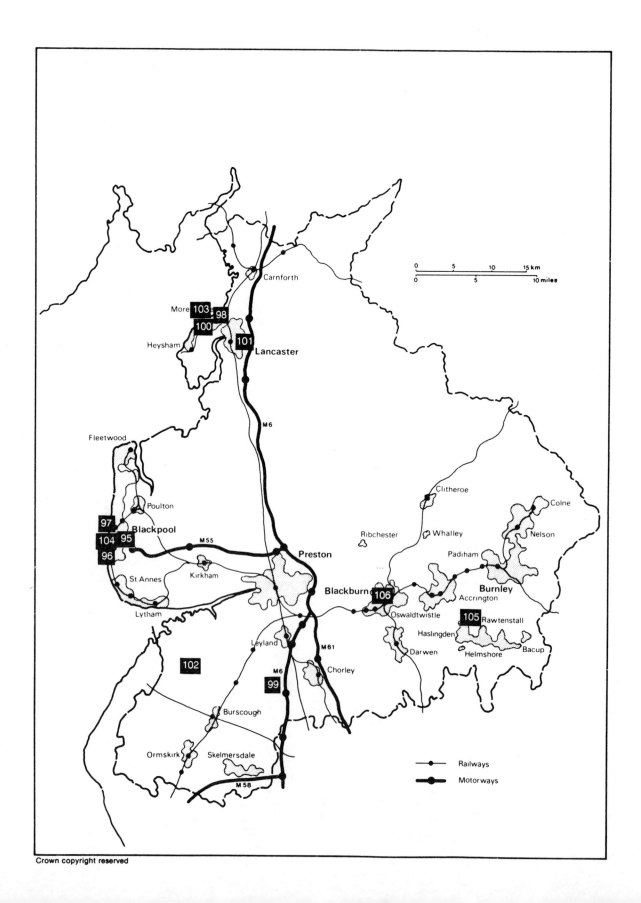

Carnforth

More 103 98
100
Heysham 101 Lancaster

M6

Fleetwood

Clitheroe

Colne

Poulton

Whalley

Nelson

Ribchester

97

Padiham

Blackpool

M55

Preston

104 95

Blackburn 106

Burnley

96

Accrington

St Annes

Kirkham

Oswaldtwistle

105 Rawtenstall

Lytham

Haslingden

Bacup

Leyland

M61

Darwen

Helmshore

102

M6

Chorley

99

Burscough

Ormskirk

Skelmersdale

Railways

Motorways

M58

0   5   10   15 km
0   5   10 miles

Blackpool Model Village

This is one of the most authentic and beautifully created model villages in Britain. All the buildings are individually styled and landscaped against a background of waterfalls, lakes, streams and over 1,500 varieties of shrubs and plants. Visitors are invited to wander at their leisure through this most colourful and unique attraction, and view all the fascinating village activities.

Admission Charges: There is an admission charge with reductions for groups.

Open: From Easter to the end of October, seven days a week, 9.30am to dusk.

How to get there 95

Location: Situated on East Park Drive, adjoining Stanley Park, approximately 2 miles from the western end of the M55 motorway which links with the M6 near Preston.

Ordnance Survey Grid Reference: SD 330 355.

Parking: Large car/coach park.

Public Transport: Bus services No.16 and 21 run regularly between the bus station and Stanley Park, and there are additional services between the seafront and the entrance to the Zoo during the summer season. A good train service operates between Preston (on the main London-Glasgow line) and Blackpool.

Contact: Model Village, Blackpool (0253) 63827.

Address: East Park Drive, Blackpool.

Facilities

Food and Drink: Tea shop, ice-cream and cold drinks on sale. Cafe nearby in Stanley Park.

Toilets: Yes.

Disabled: All inclines are graded and it is possible to bring a wheelchair around the Village.

Average Length of Stay: Up to about 1 hour.

Group Size: Any sensible size.

Leaflets/Books/Guides: Brochure on the Model Village for sale.

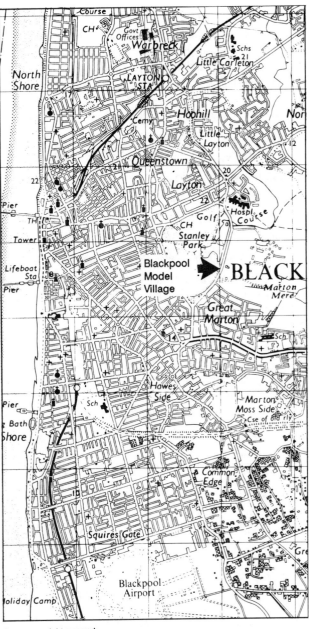

111

Blackpool Pleasure Beach

Europe's greatest amusement park, with, it is claimed, more big thrill "White Knuckle" and fun rides and attractions than any other amusement park in the world. Set in 40 acres, the Pleasure Beach has over 150 rides and attractions including The Revolution, Big Dipper, Grand National, Log Flume, Starship Enterprise, and Ranger. The Space Invader, a terrifying high speed roller coaster - in the dark. New for 1988, the Avalanche, the United Kingdom's first bobsleigh ride. There are summer season Ice Shows and Floor Shows and, for the very young, there is Funshineland and Kiddies' rides.

Admission Charges: Free to Blackpool Pleasure Beach, pay individually for rides or purchase a book of ride tickets. For shows, contact Marketing Office.

Open: Preview weekends before Easter 2pm-6pm. Easter to Spring Bank Holiday afternoons only Monday to Friday, Saturday and Sunday from 11am. Fully open from Spring Bank Holiday to end of illuminations, 11am, closing time varies.

How to get there   96

Address: Marketing Office, Blackpool Pleasure Beach, Freepost, Blackpool FY4 1BR (no stamp required).

Contact: Marketing Office.

Tel: Blackpool (0253) 41033.

Location: On Blackpool's South Shore. Leave M6 at Junction 32 and follow the M55 to Blackpool.

Ordnance Survey Grid Reference: SD 305 332.

Parking: Large car and coach park. Free coach parking for full coaches on any day throughout the season, except at weekends during the Illuminations and Bank Holiday weekends.

Public Transport: Regular train services from Preston to Blackpool South station and bus services from Preston, Liverpool, Lancaster to Talbot Road bus station, frequent tram and bus services along the seafront.

Facilities

Catering: From fast food to a la carte restaurant. Family bars, White Tower Restaurant, Seafood Restaurant, Attic Disco. Party bookings for groups of 30 to 200.

Toilets: At various locations around the Pleasure Beach.

Shelter: Covered rides and many arcades and indoor amusements.

Disabled: Toilet facilities available.

Average Length of Stay: All day.

Group Size: No limits.

Leaflets/Books/Guides: On request from the Marketing Office together with booking forms.

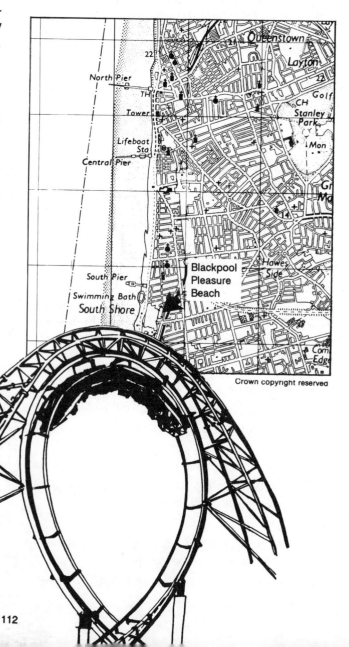

Crown copyright reserved

Blackpool Tower

One of the most famous landmarks on the Fylde coastline. The Tower is 518 feet high and contains the magnificent Tower Ballroom - generally acknowledged as one of the finest Victorian rooms in the country - with its equally famous Wurlitzer Organ. There's the Tower Dungeon, Undersea World, a children's theatre, and family showtime each evening; a Tiny Tots soft play area and Jungle Jim's adventure play place. On the fourth floor is Out of this World, Memory Lane and the lift for the Tower Top ride to enjoy unrivalled views of this popular resort.

Opening Times: End of May to early November 10am-11pm daily.

Booking Requirements: Party bookings, telephone for details.

Admission Charges: Daily admission charges vary, one ticket covers everywhere except the Circus and lounge bar.

How to get there 97

Address: Blackpool Tower, Promenade, Blackpool FY1 4BJ.

Contact: General Manager, Tower Complex. Tel:Blackpool (0253) 22242.

Location: Near to the North Pier and Blackpool North railway station.

Ordnance Survey Grid Reference: SD 305 360.

Parking: Multi-storey car park, 500 yards.

Public Transport: Regular train services to Blackpool North station and bus services to Talbot Road bus station. Frequent tram and bus services along the seafront.

Facilities

Food and Drink: Five fast food outlets, 1 restaurant, six licensed bars, "Ma Taplow's Pub".

Toilets: On every floor.

Shelter: The complex is all under cover.

Disabled: Toilet facilities for the disabled and lifts to all floors, also ramps.

Average Length of Stay: All day.

Group Size: Any size.

Leaflets/Books/Guides: Building Plan guides and souvenir brochures.

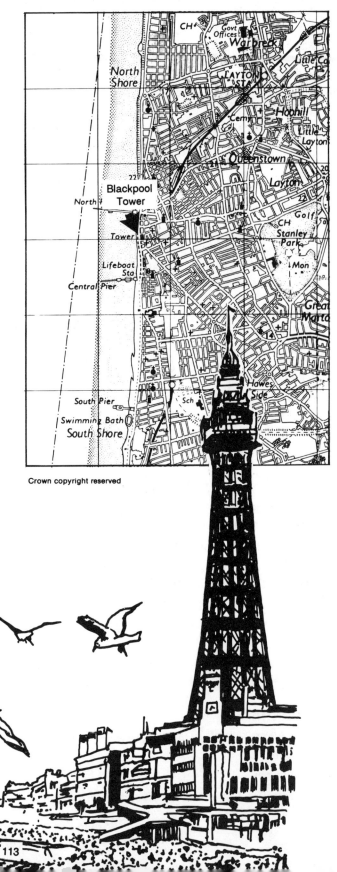

Crown copyright reserved

113

Bubbles Leisure Park and Superdome

A modern Leisure Park featuring a large heated outdoor pool - the Blue Lagoon - and cascade pool. There are terraces, sunbathing areas, games and play areas, and magnificent views across Morecambe Bay to the Lakeland Hills. Throughout the season various activities are held in the Superdome including weekly heats of the Miss Great Britain competition, cabaret nights, summer shows and concerts. Facilities at the Leisure Park complex are being upgraded and expanded and the range of activities increased.

Admission Charges: Charge is made, separate charges for evening events in the Superdome. Party rates.

Open: The Leisure Park is due to fully re-open on 9 July 1988 after extensive alterations. Hours 10am-7pm.

How to get there 98

Address: Bubbles Leisure Park and Superdome, Marine Road, Morecambe LA4 4EJ.

Contact: The Manager. Tel:Morecambe (0524) 419419.

Location: Central Promenade, Morecambe. From the M6 exit at Junction 34 and follow Morecambe signs.

Ordnance Survey Grid Reference: SD 429 645.

Parking: Public car and coach parking available nearby.

Public Transport: Frequent bus services along Promenade. Morecambe railway station is 200 yards away.

Facilities

Food and Drink: Diner take-away, licenced restaurant and bars.

Toilets: Yes.

Shelter: The Superdome, restaurants and changing rooms are under cover.

Disabled: Totally accessible for wheelchairs including deck level pool (lifeguards are in attendance). All toilets accommodate wheelchairs as do changing and showering facilities.

Average Length of Stay: All day or for specific events.

Group Size: No limits.

Leaflets/Books/Guides: Leaflet available.

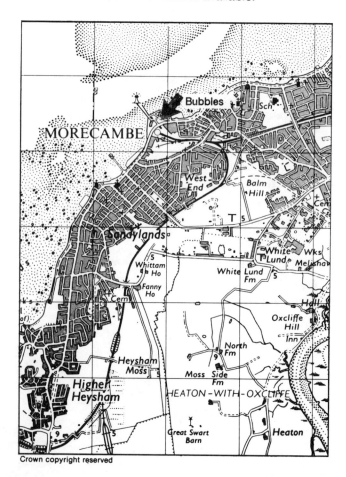

Crown copyright reserved

114

Camelot

What is claimed to be the nation's number one theme park is a magical wonderland - every child's dream - of wizards, dragons and knights in shining armour. "Camelot" is a glorious grotto set in mature parkland, with excitement around every corner for young and old alike. This year sees a greater involvement in activities for children. Merlin performs magic, there are birds of prey and a "petting zoo" where children can stroke the animals. There are rides and balloon flights and as exciting a range of fun and games that children will have ever seen.

Admission Charges: All-inclusive charge. Discount rate for parties and school groups booked 14 days in advance. Apply for details.

Opening Times: April until September 10pm to 6pm approximately. Opens Easter period, then weekends and Bank Holidays to end of May, then daily to end September, all October weekends, and school half-term.

How to get there 99

Address: "Camelot Theme Park", Park Hall, Park Hall Road, Charnock Richard, Chorley PR7 5LP.
Contact: Audrey Hatton.
Telephone: Chorley (0257) 453044.

Location: Leave M6 at Junctions 27 or 28 and follow A49; from M61 use Junction 8 for A6, B5252 and left onto A49.

Ordnance Survey Grid Reference: SD 542 157.

Parking: Extensive free parking.

Public Transport: Chorley to Croston bus service.

Facilities

Catering: Various outlets throughout the Park, two restaurants.

Toilets: On site, well signposted.

Shelter: Various rides and attractions under cover.

Disabled: Does utmost to help disabled guests to enjoy their time at "Camelot". Three sets of disabled toilets.

Amount of Time Taken: 8 hours.

Group Size: No limit. Advance booking facilities through the Guest Relations Manager.

Leaflets/Books/Guides: Various brochures and posters.

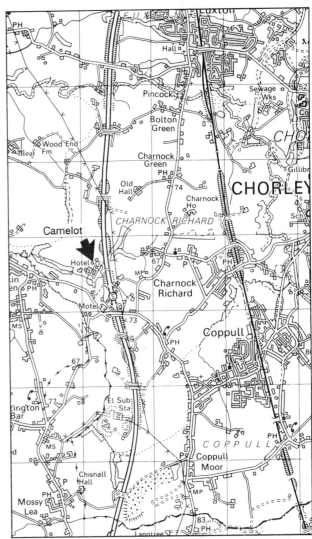

Frontierland Western Theme Park

There are over 40 thrilling rides plus live entertainment and shows in the new Country Theatre, including shoot outs, dancing, singing and magic. New Fun House. Full meals, quick snacks, family bars, picnic areas. A full range of facilities is offered for all the family to enjoy.

Admission Charges: Free admission to the Amusement Park. Day pass offers hours of fun for one price. Reduced rates for parties and for family groups.

Open: All Easter week, then weekends until Spring Bank Holiday. Then daily to the end of September, weekends only in October. Times 11am to 10pm - closing times may be varied.

Booking Requirements: Advance notice for large groups is helpful, pay on arrival.

How to get there 100

Address: Frontierland Western Theme Park, Promenade, Morecambe LA4 4DG.

Contact: Sales Promotion Office, Tel:Morecambe (0524) 410024.

Location: On the Promenade at West End, Morecambe. From motorway (M6) Junction 34 and follow Morecambe signs.

Ordnance Survey Grid Reference: SD 427 640.

Parking: Large coach and car park at the rear.

Public Transport: Frequent bus service along the Promenade. Railway station nearby.

Facilities

Food and Drink: New 500 seat restaurant - fish and chip shop - snack bars.

Toilets: Toilets in the Park and in the restaurant and licensed bars.

Shelter: Indoor arcades and numerous other attractions.

Disabled: Disabled persons regularly visit the Park. Disabled persons' toilets are available on the Park.

Amount of Time Taken: Up to a full day.

Group Size: No limits.

Leaflets/Books/Guides: Yes.

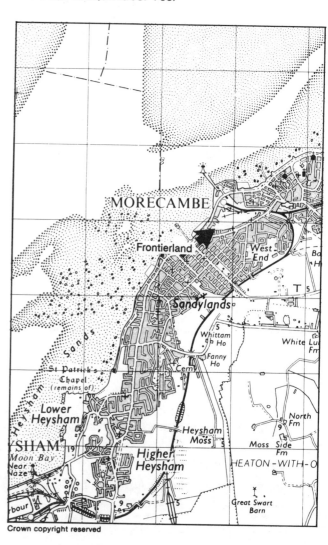

Crown copyright reserved

Lancaster Leisure Park

The Leisure Park, formerly Hornsea Pottery, is situated in 42 acres of landscaped parkland and includes 19 acres given over to the Rare Breeds Survival Unit. Children's amenities include England's longest Alpine Slide, a frontier fort and an adventure playground. Events of wide interest are held in the Park, details on application.

Opening Times: Open daily from 10am-5pm except Christmas week.

Booking Requirements: Pre-booking of meals for large groups.

Admission Charges: No charge for admission to the Park, separate charges for various children's amenities etc.

How to get there 101

Address: Wyresdale Road, Lancaster LA1 3LA.

Contact: Visits Organiser. Tel:Lancaster (0524) 68444.

Location: Approximately 1/2 mile outside Lancaster city centre, off the Wyresdale Road. 6 miles off the M6 (exit 33 or 34), and 4 miles from Morecambe.

Ordnance Survey Grid Reference: SD 488 601.

Parking: Ample free car and coach parking.

Public Transport: Bus service from Lancaster bus station.

Facilities

Catering: Extensive restaurant facilities. Pre-booked meals can be arranged.

Toilets: Yes.

Shelter: Cafe and shops under cover.

Disabled: Toilets, and ramps to all areas.

Average Length of Time Taken: Varies up to a day out for the family.

Group Sizes: No limit.

Leaflets/Books/Guides: Yes.

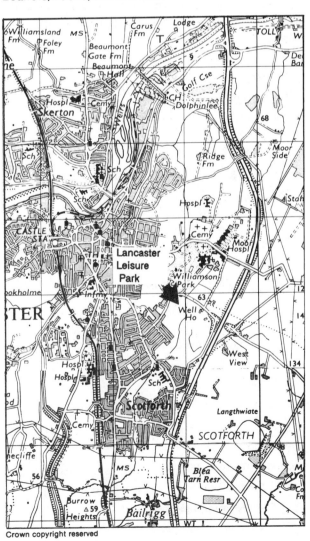

Crown copyright reserved

Leisure Lakes

A 90 acre Rural Leisure Centre based on the site of old sand workings which have been restored to form a freshwater lake with attractive sandy beaches. There is a windsurfing school, canoes and dinghies but no powered craft. Fishing is excellent and many Clubs arrange matches. There is a touring caravan park which is up to full Tourist Board specification and RAC approved. Many special events include hovercraft racing, model aircraft displays, equestrian events, country fairs and exhibitions. There is a programme of continuous improvement and extension to the facilities.

Open: 8am to 8pm.

Booking Requirements: Not normally required.

Admission Charges: Yes. Request information for special events and party bookings.

How to get there   102

Address: Mere Brow, Tarleton, near Preston.

Contact: Captain J.H. Wilson.
Tel:Preston (0772) 813446.

Location: Just off the A565 Preston-Southport road, 11 miles from Preston, 6 miles from Southport, 5 miles from Ormskirk.

Ordnance Survey Grid Reference: SD 410 178.

Parking: Large scale provision.

Public Transport: Bus services through Mere Brow on A565. Burscough New Lane railway station is 2 miles.

Facilities

Catering: Yes, including a lakeside pub.

Toilets: Yes.

Shelter: Yes.

Disabled: Provided for.

Amount of Time Taken: All day or use as a base.

Group Size: No practical limit.

Leaflets/Books/Guides: Yes.

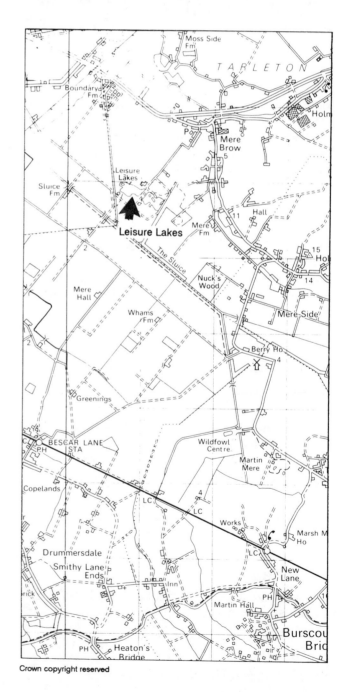

Crown copyright reserved

Marineland Oceanarium and Aquarium

The Oceanarium and Aquarium was the first of its kind in Europe. The Oceanarium has a 1,000 seat stand from which the various shows can be watched. The two pools include the deepest purpose-built dolphin pool in the country. Shows featuring dolphins and sea-lions are run continuously throughout the day. The Aquarium features turtles, alligators, tropical fresh and marine (i.e. sea-water) fish and cold water fresh and marine fish.

Open: Easter to October from 10.30am daily.

Admission Charges: Charge made for admission.

How to get there 103

Address: Marineland, Stone Jetty, Marine Road, More-cambe.

Contact: Mr. J. Braithwaite.
 Tel. Morecambe (0524) 414727.

Location: Central Promenade, Morecambe, on the Stone Jetty immediately behind the Midland Hotel.

Ordnance Survey Grid Reference: SD 427 645.

Parking: Public car and coach parking available near-by on the Winter Gardens and Empire car parks.

Public Transport: Frequent bus services along the Promenade and to Heysham and Lancaster. More-cambe railway station is 200 yards away.

Facilities

Food and Drink: Soft drinks, crisps and ice cream from kiosk.

Toilets: Toilets are available.

Shelter: The seating for the dolphin shows is under cover and the Aquarium is indoors.

Disabled: The Aquarium is easily accessible to wheel-chairs. The seating for the dolphin shows is up six steps although assistance is available for lifting wheel-chairs. Toilets do not accommodate wheelchairs.

Average Length of Stay: 30-35 minutes for dolphin and sea lion shows. Allow another hour at least for Aqua-rium.

Group Size: No limit.

Leaflets/Books/Guides: Yes. Souvenir Shop.

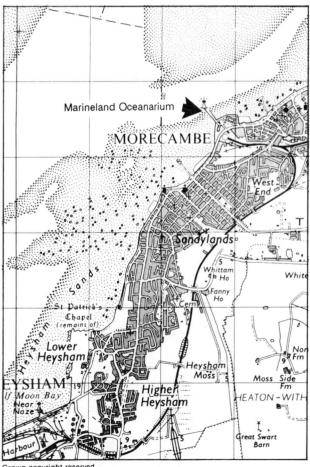

119

The Sandcastle

Three and a half acres of fun undercover. Tropical temperatures of 84F envelop four leisure pools; with wave pool, fun pool and kiddies' harbour pool plus two giant water slides with 600 feet of twists, turns and thrills and two superfast white water slides. A giant children's play area with soft play, climbing frames, bouncers, slides, pulleys, scramble nets and ball ponds. Additional facilities include seated terraces, games room, amusements arcade, sunbeds, cafes, bars and shops. There's something for all the family to enjoy at the World of Water.

Opening times: Open all year (weekends only during winter) from 10am.

Booking Requirements: Parties must be pre-booked to qualify for discount.

Admission Charges: Daily admission charges vary throughout the year. Party discounts available.

How to get there 104

Address: South Promenade, Blackpool FY4 1BB.

Contact: Sales Promoter.
Tel:Blackpool (0253) 404013.

Location: South Promenade, Blackpool. Leave M6 at Junction 32, follow M55 to Blackpool south, turn left at Promenade.

Parking: 200 space car park adjacent.

Public Transport: Frequent tram and bus services along the Promenade. Close to Blackpool South and Pleasure Beach railway stations.

Facilities

Catering: Two fast food outlets, two coffee shops, four licensed bars.

Toilets: Within the building.

Shelter: All undercover.

Disabled: Lifts and ramps to all levels. Disabled toilet, changing, shower and locker facilities.

Amount of Time Taken: Up to all day.

Group Size: No limit. Advance booking required.

Leaflets/Books/Guides: Various brochures available.

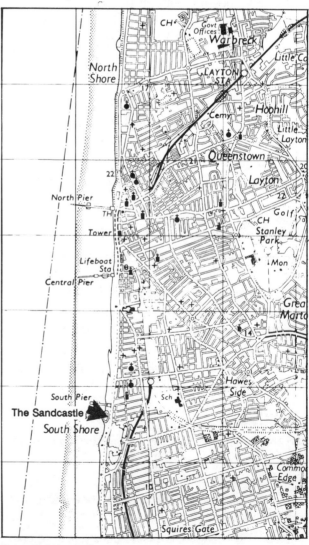

Crown copyright reserved

Ski Rossendale

Set amidst trees and parkland, Ski Rossendale commands superb views over the Rossendale Valley. The centre is ideal for beginners and experts alike. Tuition is available from qualified instructors and lessons are arranged for groups or individuals. The main slope is 180m x 12m and there are intermediate, nursery and school slopes. All slopes have ski tows and are flootlit.

Opening Times: All year round. Tuesday to Friday 10am to 10pm. Saturday and Sunday 9am to 6pm. Closed Mondays except Bank Holidays 9am to 6pm.

Booking Requirements: No booking for practice except groups 10 + . Booking normally required for tuition.

Admission Charges: Free. Charges for instruction, equipment hire.

How to get there 105

Address: Haslingden Old Road, Rawtenstall, Lancashire BB4 8RR.

Contact: Mr. Jess Baker.
Tel.:Rossendale (0706) 226457.

Location: Half a mile from centre of Rawtenstall. Half a mile from end of dual carriageway - A56/M66.

Ordnance Survey Grid Reference: SD 804 230.

Parking: Large free car park for cars and coaches.

Public Transport: Public bus service from Rawtenstall town centre. Nearest railway station Accrington. Regular bus service from Accrington to Rawtenstall.

Facilities

Catering: Licensed cafeteria, Alpine log setting; hot drinks, snacks and meals.

Toilets: In ski hire area and in cafeteria.

Shelter: Ellis Brigham ski shop, cafeteria, viewing area.

Disabled: Disabled toilet; ramp for disabled to viewing areas.

Amount of Time Taken: From one hour to all day.

Group Size: Up to 150. Groups of 10 + must book forehand.

Leaflets/Books/Guides: Leaflet. Ski books available from shop.

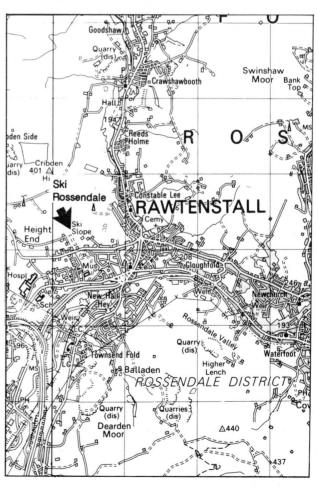

Waves Water Fun Centre

Imagine a wonderland of water, palm trees, sound and colour, where it never rains and it's never cold. A paradise for all with a blue lagoon, thrilling giant flume, Bondi wave machine, quiet play shallows and a 20-seater spa pool. That's Waves - a tropical oasis in the centre of Blackburn. Youngsters celebrate at special birthday parties entertaining their friends to a swim and a party tea. The pool's sophisticated state-of-the-art sound and light equipment make it ideal for discos. The setting is perfect for private hire for business parties, product launches, fashion shows and other trade promotions, fund raising events for charity, and "treat" visits for groups and schools. After enjoying a swim and flume rides, visitors can relax in the patio cafeteria whilst watching others enjoying themselves.

Opening Times: Monday-Friday 11am-8pm, Saturday and Sunday 10am-4pm. Opens 10am during local school holidays.

Booking Requirements: For parties 7 days in advance by telephone.

Group Size: 200 maximum.

Admission Charges: Yes; party rates available.

How to get there 106

Address: Nab Lane, Blackburn BB2 1LN.

Contact: Duncan Richardson.
Telephone:Blackburn (0254) 51111.

Location: Centrally located - corner of Nab Lane and Blakey Moor - opposite King George's Hall.

Ordnance Survey Grid Reference: SD 681 282.

Parking: Yes.

Public Transport: Town centre location.

Facilities

Catering: Cafeteria and vending machines.

Toilets: Yes.

Disabled: Changing rooms, pool and cafeteria are fully accessible.

Amount of Time Taken: As long as you want.

Leaflets/Books/Guides: Yes.

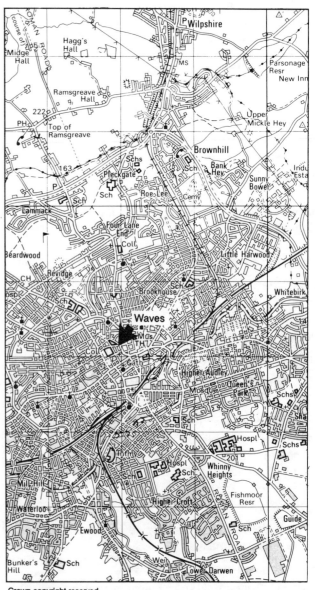

Picnic Sites

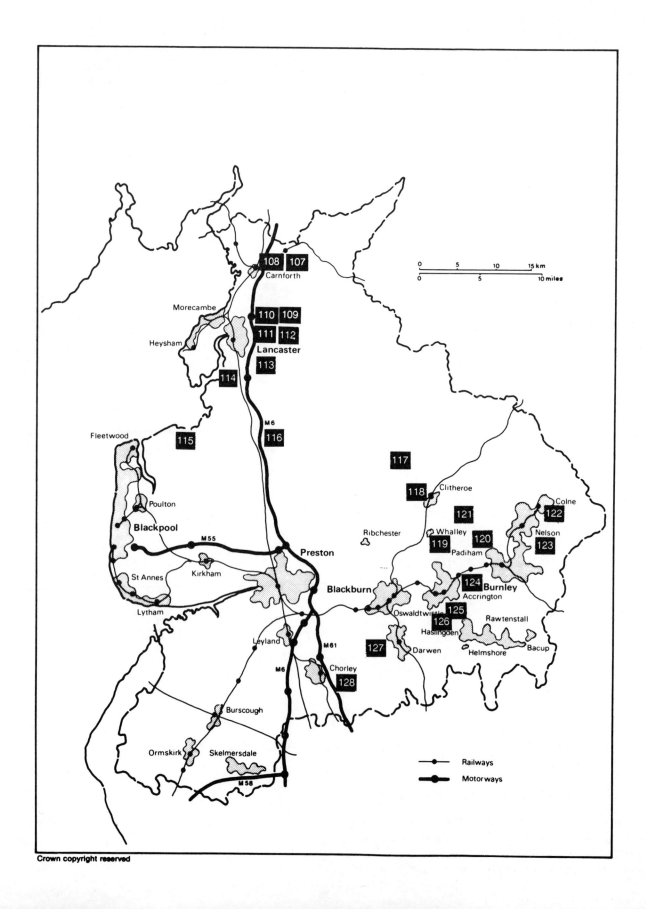

Crown copyright reserved

Thomlinson Lot Wood, Over Kellet, Lancaster 107

Small site in Forestry Commission plantation. Three miles east of Carnforth on the Borwick to Gressingham road. Ordnance Survey Grid Reference: SD 546 714.

Lord's Lot Wood, Over Kellet, Lancaster 108

Small site in Forestry Commission plantation. 3 miles east of Carnforth on the Borwick to Gressingham road. Ordnance Survey Grid Reference: SD 547 710.

Bull Beck, Caton, Lancaster 109

Popular beauty spot on the banks of the River Lune. Riverside walks. Four miles north east of Lancaster and just off A683 near Caton. Toilets with provision for the disabled. Ordnance Survey Grid Reference: SD 522 644.

Crook O'Lune, Caton, Lancaster 110

Popular stopping point near woodland and stream. Riverside walks. Toilets with provision for the disabled. In the Lune Valley alongside A683 near Caton and about 5 miles north east of Lancaster. Ordnance Survey Grid Reference: SD 542 649.

Birk Bank, Quernmore, Lancaster 111

Serves Clougha Access Area, Forest of Bowland. Viewpoint. 3 miles east of Lancaster near Quernmore. Ordnance Survey Grid Reference: SD 526 604.

Little Cragg, Littledale, Lancaster 112

Serves Clougha Access Area, Forest of Bowland. Viewpoint. 3 1/2 miles east of Lancaster near Cragg Wood. Ordnance Survey Grid Reference: SD 546 618.

Jubilee Tower, Quernmore, Lancaster 113

Serves Clougha Access Area, Forest of Bowland. Viewpoint. 3 1/2 miles south east of Lancaster and about 5 miles north west of Abbeystead. Ordnance Survey Grid Reference: SD 542 574.

Conder Green, Lancaster 114

Alongside river estuary and on the route of the Lune Estuary Coastal Path and Cycleway. Toilets with provision for the disabled. Four miles south of Lancaster just off A588 near the Stork Hotel. Half mile from Glasson. Ordnance Survey Grid Reference: SD 457 561.

Lane Ends Amenity Area, Pilling 115

Constructed on the salt marshes with walks along the tidal embankment. Half mile north east of Pilling and about 5 miles west of Garstang. Ordnance Survey Grid Reference: SD 416 494.

Scorton Picnic Site, Scorton 116

On the banks of the River Wyre, about 1 mile east of the A6 (Hollins Lane) and about 1 mile to the north of Scorton village, north of Garstang. Ordnance Survey Grid Reference: SD 505 504.

Cocklet Hill, Gisburn Forest, Slaidburn 117

Forestry Commission site in clearfelled and recently planted area near Stocks Reservoir. Four miles north east of Slaidburn. Ordnance Survey Grid Reference: SD 746 552.

Edisford Recreation Area, Clitheroe 118

Alongside the River Ribble. Riverside walks, nearby swimming baths and caravan site. About 1 mile west from the centre of Clitheroe on the B6243 - Longridge road. Ordnance Survey Grid Reference: SD 726 413.

Spring Wood, Whalley 119

Woodland setting with nature trail and pleasant walks. On A671 at junction with Whalley easterly by-pass. About 5 miles north east of Blackburn. Toilets with provision for disabled. Ordnance Survey Grid Reference: SD 742 363.

Padiham Heights, Sabden 120

Small site on high ground giving magnificent views over Sabden and Nick of Pendle. On the Sabden-Padiham road, south of the cross roads. Ordnance Survey Grid Reference: SD 787 367.

Barley Picnic Site, Barley, Near Burnley 121

Countryside Information Centre, refreshments and countryside walks. In the village of Barley close to Pendle Hill 5 miles to the north of Burnley. Ordnance Survey Grid Reference: SD 823 404.

Ball Grove, Colne 122

Children's play area, fishing lake, restaurant and toilets with provision for the disabled. Alongside Colne Water at Winewall village on the east side of Colne. Ordnance Survey Grid Reference: SD 908 403.

Thursden, Burnley 123

Small site overlooking wooded valley of Thursden Brook. Viewpoint. 2 1/2 miles to the north east of Burnley on the Haggate to Thursden Road. Ordnance Survey Grid Reference: SD 902 351.

Mill Hill (Childers Green), Burnley 124

Near small wooded area with remains of old castle. Between Accrington and Burnley and accessible off Mill Hill Lane to the south of Hapton. Ordnance Survey Grid Reference: SD 786 308.

Cocker Cobbs, Oswaldtwistle 125

Small site on a high point of the A677 with extensive views. Halfway between Blackburn and Haslingden. Ordnance Survey Grid Reference: SD 742 253.

Clough Head, The Grane, Haslingden 126

Reclaimed quarry on the Grane Road, B6232, with footpath links to Calf Hey. Large new site in the West Pennine Moors. Ordnance Survey Grid Reference: SD 752 231.

Slipper Lowe, Tockholes 127

Within the West Pennine Moors, a well wooded site with access to numerous footpaths. About 1 mile along the Tockholes Road after turning east off A675 between Abbey Village and Belmont. Ordnance Survey Grid Reference: SD 665 203.

Leicester Mill Quarries, Anglezarke, Chorley 128

Overlooking Anglezarke Reservoir with views of West Lancashire Plain. Near Rivington Country Park. Less than 2 miles east of Chorley on the road between Rivington and White Coppice. Ordnance Survey Grid Reference: SD 620 162.